"Marriage is beautiful and brutal. Marriage is brutiful. Katherine tells the truth about marriage and sets couples free to love each other imperfectly, without shame. I am so grateful for Katherine's wise, brave voice and her important work in the world."

—GLENNON DOYLE MELTON, *NEW YORK TIMES*-
BESTSELLING AUTHOR OF *CARRY ON, WARRIOR*
AND *LOVE WARRIOR*

"*Very Married* is the book we have all been waiting for: hopeful, inclusive, practical, theological, honest talk about the complex sacrament of marriage as both reality to be lived and metaphor to be embodied. Pershey is a pastor at her core, and on every page of this book, her calling is evident and wholehearted. I'm grateful for her honesty, for her wisdom, for her work in this conversation. Now when I'm asked to recommend a book about marriage, I finally have an answer: *Very Married*!"

—SARAH BESSEY, AUTHOR OF *JESUS FEMINIST*
AND *OUT OF SORTS*

"I've read my fair share of marriage books, but few are as deft in their storytelling or as honest in their reflection as *Very Married*. Pershey has written an extraordinary book, which shines an unfiltered light on the constituent parts of marriage—love, sacrifice, compromise, submission, and sex. *Very Married* does not shy away from the potential volatility of the time-honored institution, nor the God-ordained beauty of tender fidelity, and in this tension you will find its power."

—SETH HAINES, AUTHOR OF *COMING CLEAN*

"This is a marriage book I can get behind: grace-filled; doesn't take itself more seriously than it ought. It is a book on loving your spouse for 'the rest of us': regular folks working daily liturgies, choosing to witness life with the one for whom we've forsaken all others. It is a beautiful treatise on loving the gift of marriage, one I can give to friends without a second glance."
—TSH OXENREIDER, AUTHOR OF *NOTES FROM A BLUE BIKE* AND *AT HOME IN THE WORLD*

"How many adjectives am I allowed to use to wholeheartedly endorse this marvelous book? Witty, engaging, honest, thoughtful, funny, wise, nuanced, gracious. I could go on. I will read this book more than once. I will give it to many friends. And I will be forever grateful to Katherine Willis Pershey for her honest and hopeful reflection on the complex, conflicted, and glorious institution of marriage."
—AMY JULIA BECKER, AUTHOR OF *SMALL TALK* AND *A GOOD AND PERFECT GIFT*

"I thought it would take a lifetime of marriage—of bearing witness together to all the heart and heartache of being human—before I could comprehend the profound beauty of this ancient commitment. I was wrong. All it took was reading this book. What Pershey has accomplished here is mysterious and sublime. Prepare to fall in love with marriage all over again, or perhaps, even, for the first time."
—KELLY FLANAGAN, LICENSED CLINICAL PSYCHOLOGIST AND AUTHOR OF *THE MARRIAGE MANIFESTO*

"Without question, this is the most authentic, most engaging, most truthful book I've ever read about love and marriage. I intend to borrow shamelessly from this book for future premarital counseling and wedding meditations."
—KEITH GRABER MILLER, PROFESSOR OF BIBLE AND RELIGION, GOSHEN COLLEGE

VERY MARRIED

VERY
MARRIED

Field Notes on Love & Fidelity

KATHERINE WILLIS PERSHEY
FOREWORD BY EUGENE H. PETERSON

Herald Press
Harrisonburg, Virginia
Kitchener, Ontario

Library of Congress Cataloging-in-Publication Data
Names: Pershey, Katherine Willis, author.
Title: Very married : field notes on love & fidelity / Katherine Willis
  Pershey.
Description: Harrisonburg, Virginia : Herald Press, 2016. I Includes
  bibliographical references.
Identifiers: LCCN 2016024310I ISBN 9781513800172 (pbk. : alk. paper) I
  ISBN
  9781513801278 (hardcover : alk. paper)
Subjects: LCSH: Pershey, Katherine Willis. I Chrisitan biography--United
  States. I Women clergy--United States--Biography. I Marriage--Religious
  aspects--Christianity.
Classification: LCC BR1725.P453 A3 2012 I DDC 248.8/44--dc23 LC record
available at https://lccn.loc.gov/2016024310

Portions of chapters 7, 9, and 14 are reprinted with permission from the May 13, 2014, January 7, 2015, and May 1, 2015, issues of the *Christian Century*, respectively. Copyright © 2014 and 2015 by the *Christian Century*. A portion of chapter 14 was published on The Art of Simple website.

Lines from "All over Ohio" on p. 7 from *Meet Me at the Edge of the World* by Over the Rhine. Used by permission.

Maj Ragain, "A Wedding Story for Ben and Katherine," *A Hungry Ghost Surrenders His Tackle Box* (Columbus: Pavement Saw Press, 2005), 33. Used by permission.

Lines from "Order for the Recognition of the End of a Marriage," *Book of Worship* (Cleveland: United Church of Christ, 2006) All rights reserved. Used by permission.

Unless otherwise noted, Scripture text is quoted, with permission, from the *New Revised Standard Version*, © 1989, Division of Christian Education of the National Council of Churches of Christ in the United States of America.

Scripture quotations marked (ESV) are from the ESV® Bible (The Holy Bible, English Standard Version®), copyright © 2001 by Crossway, a publishing ministry of Good News Publishers. Used by permission. All rights reserved

VERY MARRIED
© 2016 by Herald Press, Harrisonburg, Virginia 22802
  Released simultaneously in Canada by Herald Press,
  Kitchener, Ontario N2G 3R1. All rights reserved.
Library of Congress Control Number: 2016024310
International Standard Book Number: 978-1-5138-0017-2 (paper); 978-1-
5138-0127-8 (hard)
Printed in United States of America
Cover and interior design by Reuben Graham.
Author photo, Marie Taylor Photography.

For orders or information, call 800-245-7894 or visit HeraldPress.com.

20 19 18 17 16   10 9 8 7 6 5 4 3 2 1

For Ben, with whom I have crossed
mountains and found home.

Love—let it be not just a feeling /
But the broken beauty /
Of what we choose to do.
—OVER THE RHINE

CONTENTS

FOREWORD

I was a pastor in a congregation for thirty-seven years. One of the tasks, both blessed and difficult, was preparing couples for marriage. Books on marriage were always a disappointment, and I gradually quit recommending them.

And then I read *Very Married: Field Notes on Love and Fidelity*. It is, without question, the very best book on marriage that I have ever read—and I have read many. If you read ten pages of this book and tell me that you set it aside out of boredom or lack of interest, I wouldn't believe you. Try me. It's incredible.

When I was still young and idealistic and a couple would come to me to prepare for marriage, we would first get acquainted through the requisite small talk. Then I would tell them that, during the weeks we conversed together, I was assigning them the task of reading *Middlemarch* by the British novelist George Eliot. I would warn them that it was a long book of nearly a thousand pages, but that reading it would be worth the trouble. I told them that I was recommending it not because it would guide them in having a good marriage, but just the opposite. Marriage at its best is a complex relationship, and every marriage is an introduction to intimacies: some delightful, others puzzling, and still others surprisingly offensive. Eliot's novel is about four couples with the best intentions in getting married who end up with terrible marriages.

I wanted to ensure that these couples knew what they were getting into and what to look out for in their good intentions in getting married. I did that for six years without a single couple reading the book. I finally got the message. *Middlemarch* was scrapped. I did as well as I could manage on my own.

I surprised myself in one of these premarital conversations by using the word *sacrifice*. A surprise because it was not a word used by Eliot, nor in any of my pastoral marriage conversations. And it was not a word that occurred in any of the marriage writings or conversations I had participated in. But it was a word I was very familiar with in meditating on Jesus' sacrificial life that released such gladness and energy into my own life.

And then I noticed the word in a poem by a friend, Jeanne Murray Walker, in her book *A Deed to the Light*. The poem used the word in a context that seemed to me to say something about marriage: "Sacrifice / is slow as a funeral procession / in rush-hour traffic, the sort of word / other words pass, honking . . ."[1]

The context released insights for me: sacrifice is to marriage what eating is to nutrition—the action that is unobtrusively transformed into holy love in the honking rush-hour traffic.

Only in acts of relational attentiveness do we realize that sacrifice is not diminishment, not a noisy "this is the cross I bear" nonsense. It results not in less joy, less satisfaction, less fulfillment, but in more—but rarely in the ways we expect.

Emily Dickinson wrote in one of her poems, "Renunciation—is a piercing Virtue."[2] And I once heard Ezra Pound, not a name we associate with marriage, quoted in a lecture: "One humane family can humanize a whole state into courtesy; one grasping and perverse man can drive a nation to chaos." The natural rivalries that develop between people who are different are countered in the act of marriage.

Even so, as I wrote in *Where Your Treasure Is*, "Marriage is an archetypal act of freedom. Marriage partners, by leaving their natural family ties, break out of networks of necessity and predictability, and at that very moment become prime movers in the politics of freedom. . . . Every marriage, then, introduces into society fresh energies of love and freedom that have the power to unself the lovers themselves but America itself."[3]

Very Married is the book I wish I had had when I was counseling soon-to-be-married couples years ago—the book that would have helped them think through the covenant of sacrifice and gladness into which they were entering. Renunciation, Dickinson's "piercing virtue," has the potential of carrying us into the long life of love, in which and by which the world will not perish.

—*Eugene H. Peterson,*
pastor, scholar, poet,
and author of The Message.

AUTHOR'S NOTE

Personal writing is subjective, and at the mercy of memory. When recounting my own stories, I aim for veracity and accuracy. I apologize for any errors I may have made.

While it's one thing for the writer to narrate her own life, it's another thing altogether for her to tell other people's stories. In order to maintain anonymity, in several instances I have changed names and altered identifying characteristics. In a very few of these instances, the mandate for confidentiality was so keen I discerned that the most ethical choice was to essentially fictionalize, preserving only the essence of stories.

That said, I assure you that my husband is indeed a ruggedly handsome redhead named Benjamin. (It would be weird to give *him* a pseudonym and an alter ego.) When my husband first read a draft of this book, I hovered nearby, anxiously awaiting his response. Appearing prominently in someone else's book would be utterly nightmarish to me; I don't know how he does it. His one and only concern about the manuscript was that I had made it sound like he was actually a John Mellencamp fan, whereas in truth he really only tolerates Mellencamp and is more of a Bob Dylan kind of guy. The only reason he went to the Mellencamp concert was because he had a free ticket. I cannot tell you how much I love this about my beloved husband, that his willingness to be vulnerable for the sake of my writing ministry stretches far and wide—but not quite so wide as to tolerate being mischaracterized musically.

This book reflects my theological convictions about marriage, which are not necessarily shared by my publisher, the denominations with which I am affiliated, or the congregation I serve. I know it's well-nigh impossible that any given reader will agree with all my conclusions about the topics at hand: at one point, I may seem to betray the liberals; at another, I risk my reputation with the conservatives. I hope it is abundantly clear how deeply I respect the other voices in the field.

Soli Deo gloria.

—*Katherine Willis Pershey*

1

WANDER AS
I WONDER

When asked if she would ever marry, Audrey Hepburn
responded, "If I get married, I want to be very married." Strictly speaking, this isn't possible. There's no differ-
ence between dead and very dead, and there is no spectrum
spanning from "sort of married" to "moderately married" to
"very married." But sometimes that which is not technically
possible is nevertheless profoundly true. I love Hepburn's
words because they are precisely how I see my own marriage.
It isn't a perfect marriage, but we are nevertheless very married. I wouldn't want it any other way.

I married Benjamin on my twenty-second birthday in the
year of our Lord 2002. We are not new at this, but neither are
we old hands; at fourteen years and counting, our marriage
is nearly halfway through its second decade. We ardently
hope to celebrate our fiftieth anniversary together. This is an

accomplishment that will require not only living that long, but living that long within the agony, ecstasy, and tedium of wedlock. Given the fragility of both life and marriage, this shall be no small feat.

I am not a marriage expert, but I am a marriage geek. Portrayals of marriage in biblical and popular literature fascinate me. I feel honored and grateful when friends and parishioners tell tales of their own marital joys and heartaches. Even my favorite bands all inexplicably end up being composed primarily of married couples; I've been obsessively listening to Over the Rhine and the Innocence Mission since the tail end of my adolescence, and the mere mention of Johnny and June is enough to make me swoon. But my interest in marriage is not merely pastoral, cultural, or intellectual. It's personal. Marriage is the fundamental fact of my life; as surely as I live and move and have my being in God, so too do I live and move and have my being within the bonds of marriage.

Many contemporary analyses of marriage are bleak, perhaps none more strikingly than the one presented by writer Sandra Tsing Loh. When she became ensnared by the allure of an extramarital affair, her "commitment to monogamy" came "unglued"—taking not only her own marriage with it, but also her respect for the entire enterprise. In an essay for the *Atlantic*, she ponders, "Now that we have white-collar work and washing machines, and our life expectancy has shot from 47 to 77, isn't the idea of lifelong marriage obsolete?"[1] At the risk of coming across like a hand-wringing church lady or a hopeless romantic, I recoil against such a proposition.

Elizabeth Gilbert had sworn off remarrying after the contentious divorce that precipitated her round-the-world recovery journey famously (or infamously, depending on whom you ask) recounted in *Eat, Pray, Love.* "You can feasibly find yourself trapped for months or even years in a loveless legal bond that has come to feel rather like a burning building," she writes in *Committed: A Skeptic Makes Peace with Marriage.* "A burning building in which you, my friend, are handcuffed to a radiator somewhere down in the basement, unable to wrench yourself free, while the smoke billows forth and the rafters are collapsing . . ."[2] Hardly a rosy testimony. Gilbert only reluctantly considered tying the knot again when marriage became the only way Gilbert, an American, and her boyfriend, a Brazilian-born Australian citizen, could live in the same place. As Gilbert goes about the business of "making peace with marriage," she exposes a seemingly endless array of pitfalls, dangers, injustices, and infelicities of the social institution. Near the end of their arduous journey toward matrimony, she came to agree with her partner's assessment of the institution: "Marriage is a game. They (the anxious and powerful) set the rules. We (the ordinary and subversive) bow obediently before those rules. *And then we go home and do whatever the hell we want anyhow.*"[3] *Committed* is maybe just a teensy bit cynical about marriage; one isn't entirely convinced Gilbert succeeds in making peace with the institution. (She and her husband have since called the whole thing off.)

Pamela Haag tosses out similarly censorious sentiments in *Marriage Confidential: The Post-Romantic Age of Workhorse Wives, Royal Children, Undersexed Spouses, and Rebel Couples Who Are Rewriting the Rules.* She's convinced that most marriages are unfulfilling at best, and slowly suffocate spirits at worst. Like Loh, Haag places the blame on an irrelevant institution: "The facts, circumstances, and the shell of marriage have changed so breathtakingly in the post-liberation era, yet the soul of marriage—its dreams, conscience, ethics, and rules—hasn't necessarily evolved to keep up."[4] Haag's critique of marriage isn't colored by an experience of divorce, but by discontentment with a marriage that apparently isn't happy enough to be satisfying nor unpleasant enough to be ended. (I found myself, as I read, occasionally cringing on behalf of Pamela Haag's better half.)

Contemporary portrayals of marriage in fiction and film aren't much sunnier. Adultery is purportedly rampant among married couples, and the film and television industry appears to honor this reality by telling countless stories of infidelity. I remember the night Benjamin and I rented *We Don't Live Here Anymore*. Based on two short stories by Andre Dubus ("We Don't Live Here Anymore" and the aptly titled "Adultery"), it is quite possibly the most depressing movie about marriage ever made. We were newlyweds and having a rough go of it thus far, so spending two hours on a Friday night watching the couples lie, cheat, and scream their way into abject misery was mildly traumatizing. A friend who watched *The Good Wife* told me that the writing and acting on the show were so deft that she discovered with some horror that she was actually rooting for the main character to have extramarital affairs. I keep waiting for writers and directors to decide that infidelity as a plot thickener is hopelessly cliché. It's not that I want fairy tales on the page and screen; I'm pleased that even Disney is edging away from the standard "then they got married and lived happily ever after" ending. (Intellectually pleased, that is. I'm apparently still an emotional sucker for a wedding just before the credits roll; I openly wept at the end of Disney's released-in-2015 yet highly traditional live-action *Cinderella*.) Still, it seems there aren't a lot of realistic and hopeful stories being told about marriage.

For all the negative depictions about marriage in our culture, it's taboo to admit publicly to anything less than marital bliss. I cheered when, during his 2013 Academy Award acceptance speech, Ben Affleck addressed his wife, Jennifer Garner: "I want to thank you for working on our marriage for ten Christmases. It's good, it is work, but it's the best kind of work, and there's no one I'd rather work with." When the camera panned to Garner, her countenance conveyed love, pain, and acknowledgment. The backlash on social media was quick and fierce; people seemed to think that he should have kept his remarks "positive," uncomplicated by nuance—even if the nuance was honest, powerful, and instructive. Affleck was expressing precisely my own experience of marriage. It is good. It is work. It is the best kind of work.

And there is no one other than Benjamin with whom I would rather work. He is a good man, my husband, possessed of what we Christians like to call a servant heart. He is funny and sensitive and humble enough that he has given me standing permission to write about him. He works in social services, and invariably earns employee recognition awards and glowing evaluations. He treats the vulnerable people he serves like people, not problems to be managed. Despite his own meaningful work, time and again he has put his career second to mine. He supported us financially while I was in graduate school, and has faced several job searches when my vocation has required relocation. For several years, when our girls were very young and childcare very expensive, he was a stay-at-home father so that I could continue working as a full-time pastor. Even though he will just laugh at me, someday I'm going to drag him to karaoke night at the bowling alley and serenade him with "Wind Beneath My Wings." It's hokey but true: my husband is as generous and supportive as they come.

My husband is also difficult. I can get away with saying this about Benjamin on account of my willingness to say this about myself. Neither of us is an easy person to live with. Perhaps if just one of us had a naturally breezy and good-humored attitude, we wouldn't have needed to spend such a sizable amount of time and energy (not to mention money) on learning to love one another well. As it is, we have both worked hard to build awareness about ourselves and one another, and to develop patience and communication skills. Even after years of practice, if we aren't mindful, his irritability and my anxiety set the tone for our marriage.

My first book, *Any Day a Beautiful Change: A Story of Faith and Family*, was supposed to be a memoir about motherhood, not marriage. But I couldn't help it. Large segments of the narrative are steeped in the trials and tribulations of our rocky first years of wedded not-quite-bliss. I wrote about the way our already strained relationship imploded after the birth of our first daughter. I wrote about how we were slowly poisoning ourselves with indignation, how I used my husband's tendency to verbally lash out as an excuse not to own up to my fair share of our problems, how we pulled off the road one afternoon and talked about the possibility of divorce while our six-month-old baby napped in her car seat. And then I wrote about how we patched it all up with a few sessions of couples therapy and a dash of prayer. By the end of the book, we were more or less living happily ever after.

Which is why I was so mortified when a misunderstanding spiraled into an enormous and ugly argument the very same day my big box of author copies arrived from my publisher.

It's not that what I wrote in that book wasn't true. It was, and is. We aren't fighting the same battles we fought before we untangled our indignations, exorcised our demons, and learned our lessons in marriage counseling. We are infinitely more mature. We communicate better. We give one another grace more readily. We still have the ability to slide into unhealthy patterns, but we know how to recognize them these days, and have a few good tricks to break out of them— including, perhaps, the most important trick of all: hope. There was a time I wouldn't have believed you if you told me that I would someday consider myself a happily married woman. There was a time I thought that ours was a marriage of two equally difficult people who would perpetually poison their love with exasperation, acrimony, and, on our worst nights, utter contempt. Yet we've learned that we can reconcile, we can forgive, we can change. But only as long as neither one of us gives up.

Sometimes the hard work of marriage isn't enough. I was waiting to pay for my eggs and asparagus when the cover of *People* magazine caught my eye and left me crestfallen: rumors of an imminent divorce between Ben Affleck and Jennifer Garner had been confirmed just one day after their tenth anniversary. I don't make a habit of becoming overly invested in the goings-on of celebrities, but I'm saddened when any marriage fails. That night at the Oscars, when Affleck hinted at the adversities of their love story, I identified with them. I rooted for them. And so, when they separated, I grieved for them.

But I don't have to look to the tabloid glossies for stories of divorce. As I was growing up, many of my friends' parents had divorced. I distinctly remember that our local public library had a bright pink book about divorce tucked into one of the spinning metal racks in the children's section. I wondered, despite my parents' seemingly stable relationship, if I would ever need to check it out. It seemed like divorce was a fate that befell some kids unexpectedly, like cancer or car accidents—you couldn't see it coming and you couldn't do anything to stop it once it did. I am now entering that stage of my life in which it is not uncommon for married friends to announce they are divorcing. It is certainly a reality I've encountered in the parish. I have observed, from my vantage point on the outside, that no matter how amicable the separation, the process of disentangling oneself from the partner one intended to live with and love for—well, *forever*—is unrelentingly awful.

While the accuracy of the statistic is contested, you'd be hard-pressed to find someone who disbelieves the conventional wisdom that 50 percent of all marriages will end. (Writer Kate Braestrup, once a young widow herself, cheerfully clarifies that *all* marriages end; if divorce doesn't separate you, death surely will.[5]) I may be optimistic, but I'm not naïve. I am acutely aware that a lot of marriages are disastrous. I know of several that presently hang by a thread, and while I hope and pray that they can be mended, it's just as likely that those last threads will fray completely. Lawyers will be retained. Custody will be brokered. Holidays will be different.

Maybe the cynics dismissing marriage are right. Why, given the risk of binding oneself to another flawed human being, would anyone take the leap? Why keep at it, Christmas after Christmas, when there is often as much drudgery and conflict—let alone pure boredom—in a marriage as there is joy and connection?

Why make the vows—and why keep them?

I am an apologist for marriage. I believe that the practice of two people entering into a lifelong monogamous relationship is worthwhile. *Good*, even. I ardently hope marriages can be saved, and that marriage as an institution can be redeemed.

I'm not alone in this hope. Evangelical Christians in particular have focused on establishing ministries intended to strengthen marriage and, in turn, families. Gary Chapman, author of the enormously popular Five Love Languages series, paved the way for many more pastors to pontificate about marriage. It seems that every megachurch pastor, from well-respected Timothy Keller to much-maligned Mark Driscoll, has penned an inspirational self-help book for heterosexual couples. (Dear reader, forgive me my unwillingness to read Driscoll's *Real Marriage: The Truth about Sex, Friendship, and Life Together*. My devotion to my research has its limits.) Ed Young, founding pastor of Fellowship Church in Grapevine, Texas, launched into the zeitgeist—and onto *The Colbert Report*—with his attention-grabbing congregational challenge and subsequent bestseller, *Sexperiment: 7 Days to*

Lasting Intimacy with Your Spouse. The program guarantees to "show you and your spouse how, over the course of
just seven days, creative sex in marriage—the way God cre-
ated it—is a tremendous catalyst that leads to much more
than a week of happiness."[6] Corollary promises include such
lofty achievements as "greater sense of purpose for your life
together" and "a lasting legacy for your future." (I cannot
help but wonder if that refers to what—or more precisely,
who—might turn up some nine months after the "sexperiment.") Yet, for all this effort to nurture and support marriage, a 2014 study from Baylor University acknowledged
that divorce rates among evangelical Christians are higher
than the national average.[7]

Many evangelical Christians have also assumed that
extending the right to marry to same-sex couples would
harm the institution of marriage they hold so dear, and have
accordingly resisted the marriage equality movement. The
culture war to prevent the "redefinition" of marriage failed
spectacularly. Affirmation of the lesbian, gay, bisexual, and
transgender (LGBT) community has surged in the last twenty
years; the degree to which public opinion has changed is
genuinely astounding. Rainbow flags flew high on June 26,
2015, as the Supreme Court ruled 5–4 that the Fourteenth
Amendment requires marriage equality. For horrified conservative Christians, the court's decision meant a blatant rejection of God's design for marriage and an attack on religious
liberty. But for the plaintiff Jim Obergefell, it meant this: his
name could be listed on the Ohio-issued death certificate of
his Maryland-married husband, who died in 2013. For those
who support marriage equality—and I count myself among

this crowd—this ruling was not an assault on the sanctity of marriage but a just and rightful expansion of it. In the final paragraph of the majority opinion, Justice Anthony Kennedy declared, "No union is more profound than marriage, for it embodies the highest ideals of love, fidelity, devotion, sacrifice, and family. In forming a marital union, two people become something greater than once they were."[8] Amen.

I sympathize with my friends who are loving and unbigoted people whose theological and biblical interpretations lead them to believe that marriage is only valid between a man and a woman. I know firsthand that it is disconcerting to see your culture and your country part ways from your convictions. But on that historic day, I cheered for my exultant gay and lesbian friends. Their families were no longer second-class, no longer vulnerable to the variations of state laws. Their relationships had long made them something greater than what they once were, but through *Obergefell v. Hodges*, they became legally protected, possessed of all the same privileges, rights, and responsibilities as their heterosexual counterparts.

Without denying that for some people marriage is more like being trapped in a burning building than being sustained by a holy covenant, I rather enjoy that in marriage we mix love and legalities, sex and housekeeping, church and state. When married people experience temptation, I think they should flee from it. When married people experience conflict, I pray they can work through it. When married people get into bed at night, I hope they can get jiggy with it. Sandra Tsing Loh suggests that since one's commitment to monogamy can be unglued, why not dismantle the whole thing? And I go on a quest for more glue.

My love for marriage is much like my love for religion—not just faith or spirituality, but *religion*. The root word for *religion* means "to bind." To connect. The word *ligament* derives from the same word. There are some folks who think it's best to be unbound, that to be free is to be completely independent. But ask someone who has experienced the pain of a torn ligament if his flesh is better off disconnected; I think not.

In *An Altar in the World*, Barbara Brown Taylor makes the case that one of the most spiritually resonant questions one can ponder is this: *What is saving my life right now?* Frankly, the first time I encountered the query, I was confused. Wouldn't the perennial answer, for a confessing Christian, be *Jesus*? Yes, in a way. But the grace of God is malleable and industrious. It takes the form of God's only begotten Son in a singular and glorious way, but it also takes the form of birdsong, text messages, freshly baked bread, the intervention of a wise friend. When I answer that question honestly, often what is presently saving my life is my marriage. It is an institution, but it is also a means of grace.

Our lives are saved time and again; maybe our marriages are as well. I am an apologist for marriage, but I will not impose on the reader a well-intentioned but inherently limited argument for how we should save it. Rather, I will consider how the love Benjamin and I have for each other has flourished and where has it floundered. I will rejoice in the ways the vows of our marriage covenant have made us free and in the ways they have benevolently yanked us away from peril.

I will pay attention to the winds of culture and the words of Scripture. I will contemplate the history and theology of marriage as I seek to better understand this most intimate of unions. I will share stories that are not my own but that I have received dispensation to retell. I will bear testimony to the grace of God as it is made manifest in the making of a life, together. I will wander as I wonder what is saving my marriage right now.

2

IN WANT OF
A HUSBAND

My husband has long joked that I must have married
him for love, because I sure as heck didn't marry him
for his money. He was flat broke when we started dating.
The hourly wage for his night shifts at a local group home
for people living with mental illness wasn't enough to cover
much more than rent and bare essentials, so each month his
credit card debt inched a little higher. My own finances were
less dicey, but only because my emerging adulthood was gen-
erously underwritten by my parents. (I am *such* a millennial;
my husband, more than five years my elder, is so very generation X.) I recall more than a few squabbles about Benjamin's
infuriating habit of selling off his CD collection. I knew I
wasn't marrying into wealth; I at least wanted to marry into
the complete discography of Whiskeytown, Jeff Buckley, and
Iris Dement. It took me forever to realize that he *needed* the

five bucks each disc netted at the Record Exchange to help pay off my amethyst engagement ring, which cost a whopping seventy-five dollars at the Antique Jewelry Mall. His economic potential wasn't exactly impressive, either. Because he'd dropped out of college before we met and didn't have a trade to fall back on, his employment prospects were limited. No, I did not marry for money.

From the outside looking in, our whirlwind courtship was irrationally and impetuously romantic. Just three months after he took me out for a late August dinner, we got engaged, setting a wedding date for the following summer.

Yes, we fell in love, and love was surely a primary reason we filled a sanctuary with our friends and family to publicly declare our intention to spend the rest of our lives together. But it was far from the only reason.

Not long ago I asked Benjamin why he had wanted to marry me. He loved me, of course, and still does. But he also admits that the fact I loved him and wanted to marry him might have been sufficient to provoke his reciprocal affections. Adulthood hadn't been especially easy for him. There he was, figuratively "unemployed in Greenland," if you'll pardon the *Princess Bride* reference. At twenty-six, he had a handful of smart and funny friends but little by way of a love life. He'd spent time in and out of rehab since his early twenties; when we first met in a poetry class, I was a fresh-faced sophomore, and he was living at a halfway house where he was trying, and largely failing, to get sober. By the time we reconnected a couple of years later, his life was somewhat more stable, but depression, loneliness, and the impulse to drink himself to oblivion still dogged him.

Benjamin can be a shy guy, too shy to risk asking me out to dinner on the phone or in the flesh. He found an excuse to issue the invitation in writing when I traveled to Mexico for a summer study-abroad program. I reread the letter in my hotel room in Teotihuacán. I'd ventured there alone, to explore the city and write. I reckon I didn't compose a single poem that weekend, having spent all my best words penning the perfect reply. When I wrote back to say yes, I was responding with a much bigger yes than he could have imagined. I intuitively knew that if we went on that first date, we would end up getting married—and soon.

In truth, I didn't merely intuit this. I all but planned it. I've pondered the possibility that ours is something of an arranged marriage after all—not in the traditional way, in which future inlaws make the match and negotiate the terms of engagement. I did the arranging myself, trusting that the love would keep apace of the commitments.

Why the designs on this particular man? After all, he wasn't the easiest "sell" to my parents. Their youngest daughter, a twenty-one-year-old honors student, engaged to a college dropout with a drinking problem? Even my Mexican host mother clucked her tongue when I described the boy eagerly awaiting my return to the States. And yet I was deeply drawn to Benjamin. I knew him to be a fundamentally decent person, beneath the lack of conventional success. The poems he read at the local poetry readings we frequented revealed a tender and principled heart. He was paradoxically a bad boy *and* a good guy, and therefore irresistible to a girl who couldn't decide which one she preferred. Furthermore, though it sounds terribly manipulative to admit this, he was ripe for the picking, altogether vulnerable to the attentions of a girl such as myself.

My attentions weren't sinister in nature. I meant well, for him and for me. Frankly, I'm not sure how much of this was even above a subconscious level. But lo, these many years later, I can see with impeccable hindsight what I was up to. I fancied the notion of being *his* knight (knight-ess?) in shining armor.

When we were newly dating—just a few weeks after the Twin Towers were felled in New York City—we drove across Ohio and Indiana to Chicago for a momentous weekend. In addition to my appointments with the admissions directors of a few graduate schools in Hyde Park, we were also to meet one another's friends. I introduced Benjamin to my friend Christopher; Christopher had been my date to the eighth-grade dance and the giver of my first kiss. We broke up not long after our freshman homecoming dance but remained good friends, and might have even rekindled our romance if not for our irreconcilable theological differences. He was a student at the conservative Moody Bible Institute, while I was considering applying to the University of Chicago's liberal divinity school.

I don't know why I wanted those two young men in the same room. I might have subconsciously wanted to see how the new boyfriend stacked up against the old—not in physical appearance or even personality, but in gravitas. Christopher meant a lot to me, but he struck me as safe to the point of insubstantial. He was so innocent and earnest, so unwounded. He didn't question or agonize or ever speak impolitely to his mother (or anyone else, for that matter). I already thought of Benjamin as a person of depth and danger. I played the Cowboy Junkies' "Misguided Angel" on repeat that fall. Benjamin was wounded in a way that struck me as deeply sexy. He was the antithesis of the boy whose name I used to scribble in my journal, the boy I claimed was too fundamentalist but might have simply been too nice.

The meeting was awkward, unsurprisingly, especially when we joined Benjamin's friends for a night out at an experimental theater company. Maybe things have changed, but back then, Moody Bible Institute kids did not, as a matter of course, attend experimental theater productions. After the show, as we walked culture-shocked Christopher back to the relative safety of his no-girls-allowed dorm room, we chatted with Steve, Benjamin's best friend and former roommate. Christopher and Steve had so little in common that the only thing they could talk about was us. Steve said it would take a special woman to be with Benjamin. I glanced at Benjamin as he coughed up a fake laugh and fell into a sullen, stony silence that lingered for the rest of the evening. He received Steve's words as a heartbreaking insult, an embarrassing admission that he was hard to live with.

I, on the other hand, was flattered. I wanted to be a special woman. Moreover, I heard what Benjamin couldn't hear: the other half of the remark, the affirmation that loving him was worth it. It was a perfect letter of reference.

In addition to saving him from himself, I suspected he could save me, too. While I enjoyed the weekend in Chicago, I had a hankering to go someplace far away from my native Midwest, preferably someplace warm. A seminary in Los Angeles County had dangled a sizeable scholarship in my direction, but I was straight up scared to set off on my own. Perhaps a more confident young woman would have relished an unfettered season, as an increasing number of millennials do; the average age of individuals marrying for the first time has skyrocketed in the last few decades. For me, however, the idea of being a swinging single had absolutely no appeal, not even in sunny Southern California. I longed for security and companionship, for someone who would do most of the laundry and all of the driving. I was also eager to escape the agonizing quandary of premarital sexuality, a perennial source of stress and shame.

I was in want of a husband: someone to have and to hold, for richer or poorer, in sickness and in health. One morning, a mere three months after our first date, we met at St. Patrick's on Depeyster Street, where Benjamin liked to go to daily mass at the end of his night shift (for a "nonpracticing" Catholic, he got a lot of practice). I knew what was in his pocket. After the benediction, when he lowered the kneeler, I knew he was not getting on his knees to pray.

We chuckled at the convenience—how many proposals involve such a highly functional prop? He asked the question and I gave the answer, and together we slipped the amethyst engagement ring past my knuckle. And then we left, wondering if the handful of solitary worshipers had noticed anything as they shuffled out of their pews. We celebrated our engagement with scrambled eggs and biscuits at Bob Evans, after which we made a few phone calls to inform our mildly dazed friends and family members, many of whom were only vaguely aware we were even dating. Benjamin crashed on his futon and I rushed to my senior seminar.

I would marry this man, and we would go west together. I would marry this man, and neither of us would languish alone. "Misguided angel, love you 'til I'm dead," I sang in the shower. "California dreamin' on such a winter's day," I hummed in the car.

Yes, we loved one another. But we also needed one another, and married as much out of practical aspirations as romantic ones. For a good long while I repressed this reality. It seemed wrong, somehow, to have ulterior motives for marriage in a culture that lauds one reason alone as a legitimate impetus to tie the knot: true love. People marry for money, insurance benefits, green cards, and other nonromantic pursuits, but they generally do so under at least the pretense of love.

In *Marriage, A History: How Love Conquered Marriage*, social historian Stephanie Coontz traces the extraordinary transformations of marriage over the course of thousands of years. To the abject horror of my two young daughters, who have been sternly trained not to write in books, I filled the margins of Coontz's masterpiece with notes and exclamation points. Though I knew the rise of so-called love marriages was a relatively recent phenomenon, I was ignorant of the complicated history of the institution. In the grand sweep of history, far fewer marriages have been brokered for love than over such issues as economics, security, pregnancy, parental pressure, and the formation of inlaw networks. There isn't consensus as to how marriage was invented. Though the Judeo-Christian tradition points to the garden of Eden as the metaphorical if not literal genesis of marriage, anthropologists have wondered if marriage began as a trade of "meat for sex"—the man providing sustenance and protection in exchange for getting some action in the darkest corner of the cave. But most researchers have concluded that the theory doesn't really hold—at least not universally. For one thing, prehistoric married couples didn't sequester themselves the way contemporary families tend to do. Resources and responsibilities weren't split between a couple, but shared by the whole tribe. Marriage was less about nurturing a cozy relationship between two lovers than establishing kinship alliances between different bands of hunter-gatherers. As distasteful as it is to think of women as pawns in tribal transactions, the exchange of marriageable women—and girls—was central to the development of civilization.

Before long, marriage also became a means of accumulating wealth and power, and the selection of a spouse became ever more a matter of economics. Even marriages among the poorer classes were driven by decidedly nonromantic motives. The practice of a young man or young woman autonomously deciding who he or she would marry was simply unheard of. Marriage was for the parents of the bride and groom to arrange. Undoubtedly, some parents were more open to their offspring's personal feelings on the matter, but legally and culturally, it was presumed that "Father knew best."

The predominance of the love marriage in the West is a mere two centuries old, give or take a few years. Before the Victorian era, marrying for love was considered irresponsible. How could something so critical to the social order be left to the auspices of hormonal and impetuous young people? Surely, if given free rein to marry whomever they chose, they would choose poorly.

Free rein, however, is a relative term. As the case for marriages galvanized by love expanded autonomy in matrimonial selection, the leash got only so long; prohibitions against certain marriages were still legally binding. If you were a white woman in love with a black man, for instance, you were out of luck. Antimiscegenation laws weren't counted as unconstitutional until as recently as 1967, when Mildred and Richard Loving won their case in the Supreme Court. (This is such recent history that my own parents were already married by then.) Richard Loving had sent, through his lawyer, a declaration of love and a plea for justice: "Tell the court I love my wife, and it is just unfair that I can't live with her in Virginia."[1]

The church's position on marriage—who people could marry, and for what reasons—has also morphed immensely over the centuries. Many early Christians considered marriage an inferior status. Celibacy was the preferred state for believers. In his first letter to the Corinthians, Paul encouraged the unmarried to remain unmarried. Yet as Christendom emerged, granting the church political heft and a say in the formation of social norms and sexual mores, the church's role shifted to monitoring rather than denouncing marital unions. Before long the church became intimately embroiled in the marriages—and divorces—of political leaders throughout Europe. Coontz reports, unsurprisingly, that the church did not always use its power with integrity. In the Middle Ages, she writes, "church officials tracked down the participants in marital disputes, hounded them for details of their sex lives, and became partisan advocates for one party or another."[2] For a spell, ecclesiastical policies were fixated on the matter of incest, defining it so broadly that it was hard to find anyone eligible to become one's spouse—and easy to uncover that an unwanted spouse was actually one's eighth cousin. Three cheers: such a discovery made perfect grounds

for annulment! King Henry VIII famously founded the
Church of England when he was fed up with the pope's vise
grip on marriage. If it took a schism to come by a divorce—
freeing him to marry Anne Boleyn—so be it.

The church was not merely concerned with royal matrimony. The marriages of ordinary folks were also governed
partly by an ever-evolving ecclesial authority. While marriage
was once a matter of a bride and groom making vows, with or
without witnesses, it became, over time, a complicated ritual
requiring parental consent, a dowry, public announcements,
and the presence of a priest. All these elements served as bar-
ricades to autonomy, making clear that marriage was a *social*
institution, despite its profoundly personal consequences.
Even as the church loosened these requirements and adapted
to the rise of the love marriage, not every couple seeking a
pastor's blessing was able to receive it. "Mixed" marriages
between Catholics and Protestants still require special dis-
pensations from the Roman Catholic Church. Many clergy
still refuse to officiate at the weddings of interfaith couples,
or couples who live together before marriage, or couples who
are of the same sex—although it should be pointed out that
many of these clergy *might* officiate such marriages if their
denominational policies allowed them to do so.

None of this was on my mind when Benjamin and I signed
up for the premarital counseling sessions required by my
temporary church home. Though I'd grown up in one tradition (United Methodist) and intended to seek ordination in
another (Disciples of Christ), during college I'd worked as a
youth minister at Christ Episcopal Church of Kent, Ohio, and
I'd grown fond of the place. I liked the priest and loved the

Book of Common Prayer; the liturgies for Sunday mornings were beautiful, and the language of its wedding ceremony was pure poetry. These, it seemed, were reasons enough to be married there.

I didn't know the complex background linking the institutions of church and marriage, or that the historical role of clergy had often been to be the gatekeepers of matrimony. Still, as we walked into Rev. Hamilton's study in the modern addition recently tacked onto the traditional sanctuary, I felt as if I were going into a professor's office for an oral examination. We had to prove that we were worthy of wedlock. I can't recall much about those meetings except that I was very clearly putting on a show. *We are mature! We are made for one another! We have a realistic understanding of the vicissitudes of married life!*

I was relieved when, at our last session, the priest leaned back and crossed his arms. We'd do just fine, he decreed, and given that we neither drank nor smoked nor—at least for the time being—ate meat, we wouldn't even have to worry about money. (For the record, Benjamin's vegetarianism lasted a matter of days. Perhaps even a matter of meals. Mine lasted until I finally surrendered to the invariable meatiness of church potlucks.)

We had passed the ecclesial examination. We still needed the blessing of the civil authority, but with our privilege as a heterosexual couple, procuring the marriage license simply required our presence, birth certificates in hand, at the county courthouse. Call the florist and book the honeymoon: the nuptials were on.

3

THE BINDING
THAT BOUND US

I wore a pink lace dress that I bought for a song; Benjamin's tailored pinstripe suit was the sartorial investment. We thought he could wear it to job interviews when we settled in Los Angeles, not comprehending that you have to be fairly high in the employment echelon to require a tailored suit in California. I insisted that we walk down the aisle together, hand in hand. I didn't want to be "given away," even if the priest softened the traditional words indicating a patriarchal transaction from father to husband. I presented myself for marriage. I never asked my father if this disappointed him— if my unevenly applied feminist principles robbed him of a poignant moment with his daughter. I do, in retrospect, sense that I robbed myself of a poignant moment with my father.

Thanks to the invention of Pinterest, weddings these days are increasingly unique. Our wedding predated Pinterest, so even though I had aspirations toward bromide-busting self-expression (exhibit A: the aforementioned pink dress), I had no frame of reference for a wedding without, say, the obligatory unity candle, that newfangled yet widespread symbol of marital union. There were few surprises during our wedding ceremony. The priest intoned, "Dearly beloved, we are gathered here today . . ." An old friend read 1 Corinthians 13, as an old friend customarily does at these things. We joined hands and spoke timeless vows, voices wavering with nerves and emotion. Even if I had the entirety of Pinterest at my fingertips, I wouldn't have covenanted myself to a husband with anything less than vintage vows. I wanted not merely to repeat the words of the priest in his vestments. I wanted to echo the words that have been uttered at altars for centuries.

For all the conventional trappings of our wedding, I was surprised twice in the course of the ceremony. The first unexpected moment is apparently common in Episcopal weddings, but the jolly priest had failed to mention it during our wedding rehearsal. After our silver wedding bands were produced from the best man's pocket, blessed, and slipped onto our respective fourth fingers, Rev. Hamilton began winding his white wedding stole around our still-clasped hands. When he finished, we were fastened to one another, but also to him; the stole still hung from his neck, making us an odd, awkward, and wholly unexpected trinity. It was in that moment—flustered, confused, and literally tied up—that the priest declared us husband and wife. More than a laughably extinguishable flame, more even than rings forced over swollen and sweaty fingers, it was the binding that bound us. Wrapped in God's

blessings, we were married. In the first moment of our marriage, we had already learned that marriage was more than
we bargained for.

And then there was the poem. The poetry class that
brought Benjamin and I to the same conference table was
taught by a man named Maj Ragain, a man we both love.
Maj—which appropriately rhymes with *sage*—is a grizzled
and gracious Midwestern giant; it hardly seems plausible that
his great spirit fits into a frame truncated by childhood polio.
He does not walk anymore, though when we met him he did,
painstakingly, with old wooden crutches. When we visit him
on our trips back home to Ohio, our daughters delight in this
rare grownup who receives visitors from his favorite spot on
the thick woolen rug covering his living room floor, barrel
chest propped up by his burly arms.

But that day there were not yet daughters, and his crutches
had not yet failed to be sufficient. While we sat expectantly in
the first pew, Maj made his way to the chancel with a lengthy
poem stuffed in the pocket of his jacket. The poem was an
original, written for us by request—*my* request, to the mortification of my intended. Benjamin is not the kind of person who would request the composition of an original poem,
even from a poetry professor as beloved and dear as our Maj.
I, on the other hand, will make the tacky ask.

Maj looked out at the people before he began to read.
His gaze wasn't set for appraisal; rather, it was an expression of acknowledgment and humility, an expression intent
on honoring those who would pay him the gift of attention.
I'd seen the look before, in class and at the coffeehouse. This
time, however, he nodded not at a bunch of undergrads or

poetry-loving townies but at our wedding guests: my grandmother, the men who lived in the group home where Benjamin worked, our parents, and siblings and friends. Maj cleared his throat. "A Wedding Story for Ben and Katherine."

The poem was for us but not about us. The poem was about Afzal, a Russian orphan who had been adopted by Maj's friends Daniel and Margaret. The story went like this: Afzal's life began in a lonely orphanage in Tobolsk, where he lived for nearly two years until Daniel and Margaret journeyed from the other side of the world to bring him home. The poem described the afternoon Afzal and his parents visited Maj and his wife, LuAnn, at their house in Kent. Midway through the afternoon, a leaky diaper called for the use of a coiled green garden hose. The toddler played joyously in the sprinkler until he discovered how much more fun he could have by commandeering the spray and turning it on the adults.

I don't really have to tell you that I wasn't expecting our wedding poem to include these lines: "He gallops through the / upside down rain, the silver lattice, butt / bare, his laughter and straight ahead pecker pointing the way back and forth through the water, / in the sunshine fall from whatever heaven / there is, in the grace of things as they are." Some of the wedding guests surely blanched. I loved it.

Maj being Maj, I should have expected that the wedding poem would be written at a slant. But Maj being Maj, I fully expected the wedding poem to be infused with wisdom, and it was. After the gloriously raunchy opening scene (the leaky diaper was noted by the "trickle of skyline chili down the back / of his leg"), the poem turned to us.

None of us knows the source of the splendor
that spills over us everyday.
Ben and Katherine, take your dousing.

Refuse the towel. Stay wet.
When you don't know what else
to do, bow your head.

It is your gift to others.
The clarity of the heavens, the milky river
of stars, all look down on the backyard mud
where Afzal dances.
Where you are is more than you want.

Everywhere is darkness, save small lanterns
hung here and there in immense, cold chambers.
Make a bonfire together.
Be warmed by the burning of old and new found
stupidities.

To pledge your troth means to put
your truth in peril. Attend to the unfolding.
You have come a long way to stand here together.

Find a failing in the other you cannot
bring yourself to love. Befriend that.
It is a secret door that opens into
a garden.

It is all God's work, the watermelon's sunset
split open, the miracle of bread, the play
of rainbow light through the spray. There is
a present glory in raising the fingers to the lips.

Never forget Afzal, now John Carter Afzal Bourne,
another of the best men, one day in a Siberian
orphanage, at a long table waiting for the bread
to make its way down the long line of hands,

faces and empty plates. The next day he is
in the arms of a father and a mother, carried
home over snowy mountains, across an ocean.
That is the way it is. Trust what has chosen you.

Untangle the old knots. Someone else tied those
for you. Tie this new one here, together, today.

Ben and Katherine, enter this marriage as if
you are crossing great mountains
and going home.

The poem washed over me. I knew I would need a lifetime
to understand it, a lifetime bound to the one with whom I
would literally and figuratively cross mountains, a lifetime
tied to the one with whom I would make a home.

4

IF I KNEW THEN

The wedding night was a revelation, an awkward yet wondrous consummation of physical and emotional yearning. The bride and groom had carefully tended their virginity so as to give one another a wedding gift of extraordinary significance. In the months before the wedding they would make out for hours, all but consumed by the force of their desire for one another. Their lips might have been rendered raw from kissing, but they assiduously respected the boundaries they had together discerned were appropriate, the boundaries that honored the commitment they had made to themselves and to God. As their wedding approached, they were not only enthusiastically looking forward to all the trappings of ceremony and reception. They were enthusiastically looking forward to the sex.

Sarah Jane leaned back in the vinyl-upholstered booth in apparent reverie, savoring both the uncommonly good airport food and the retelling of her wedding night. I had coaxed the story out of my friend while we waited for our respective flights over breakfast quesadillas in the food court. Truth be told, it didn't take much coaxing. It was a story worth telling, but not the sort of story you just casually toss out at a dinner party. She didn't blush or stammer as she spoke. She did not speak of pride that she had crossed the finish line to matrimony, virginity intact. She simply radiated a tender, timeworn joy as she remembered.

Benjamin was not my first. Not my first love, and not my first . . . *first*. Although I once was the proud wearer of a purity ring—a silver band acquired in junior high school that advertised my intention to remain a virgin until my wedding night—at some point along the way, I misplaced the ring, and some years later, the virginity.

Beyond bursting into tears in the bathroom when it was over, I have few memories of the first time I went "all the way" with a boyfriend. The ring may have been gone, but I had absorbed its message. Sexual activity beyond the boundaries of marriage was wrong—a sin. Possibly even worse to a teenager acutely aware of peer pressure, the sexual relationship made me an outlier among my friends. They were good girls. They knew how to say no. At one point, a well-behaved and conscientious friend even ratted me out to her mother. Her mother, a friend of the family, called me up on the telephone after school one day to confront me. Never before or since have I experienced such an intense embarrassment as the afternoon I was lectured about touching a boy's penis. The only reason I didn't hang up on her or dissolve into a nonverbal puddle of mortification was my burning desire to get a word in edgewise: *Please, please, please, Mrs. Callahan, don't tell my mother.*

I had sex before I was married even though in his first letter to the Corinthians, Paul writes that "if they are not practicing self-control, they should marry. For it is better to marry than to be aflame with passion." I had sex before I was married even though practically every issue of my beloved *Brio* magazine managed to communicate that this was the worst possible thing a girl could do. I had sex before I was married even though I felt deeply guilty for everything I did, up to and including actual intercourse. Kissing and French kissing, petting and French petting (is that a thing?): it all filled me with a shame that overwhelmed whatever pleasure I might have otherwise derived.

Shame and gender norms notwithstanding, I pushed for more. With a few exceptions, I was often the instigator of the make-out sessions and the buyer of the condoms. I was a typically hormonal adolescent and young adult, after all, and hormones are a potent force. Yet as I recall the dalliances of my younger days, it's clear that sexual desire was only partly responsible. Curiosity kills the cat and lures the lusty. Part of my desire was a desire to *know*. I wasn't hungry for the apple as much as the mystery shrouded by its shiny red veneer. It makes all the sense in the world to me why the biblical idiom for sex is *knowing*; to know a man is to have been to bed with him.

As a girl hungry for God, I was drawn to Christian boys. Naturally, I proceeded to play the role of the fallen woman, taking the innocent and unsuspecting male down with her. I once fell deeply in love with a charismatic, handsome, and narcissistic man. At the time I thought he was wondrously inscrutable and mysterious. Now I suspect he was actually just hypocritical and emotionally unavailable. One night he casually mentioned that he wanted to marry a virgin.

We had *just* had sex.

I was naked and ashamed. The depth of rejection and betrayal I felt might have awoken me to the brokenness of our pairing, but I was far too consumed by the relationship. I felt no anger at the egregious double standard; it did not dawn on me to be vexed that he didn't seem as concerned about his *own* lack of virginity as he was about that of his ideal future wife. I didn't want out of his arms. I wanted to be redeemed so he would have me again. After an awkward silence, we untangled our bodies, got dressed, and then, at his suggestion, we prayed for forgiveness for having surrendered to the temptations of the flesh. We may as well have crossed our fingers as we promised Jesus that we wouldn't do it again.

While many biblical passages imply that marriage is the appropriate context for sexual activity, the prohibition against unmarried sex has been proclaimed even more loudly by the Christian church. Some historical epochs have been less forgiving to illicit lovers than others. Woe to the maiden Puritan who turned up pregnant in the seventeenth-century New England Colonies. Woe, too, to the evangelical Christian who had premarital sex in the 1990s. A few years ago, my friend Sarah Bessey practically broke the Internet with her viral blog post "I Am Damaged Goods." In her essay, she recounts an object lesson popular within a particular subculture of evangelical Christianity. In the midst of an impassioned lecture condemning sinners who had given in to lust, her youth pastor passed around a glass of water, encouraging the boys in the audience to spit into it. Upon daring someone in the crowd to drink the cocktail, the disgusted young people were charged to consider the cup the equivalent of an unmarried yet sexually active person. "This is what you are like if you have sex before marriage . . . you are asking your future husband or wife to drink this cup."[1]

Bessey rejects the narrative. She refuses to accept the message that her worth is tied up in her sexual status. She preaches to herself and to me and to all who need to hear a good and gracious word spoken into their secret shame: "For I am convinced, right along with the Apostle Paul, that neither death nor life, neither angels nor demons, neither the present nor the future, nor any other power, neither height nor depth, nor anything else in all creation, will be able to separate us from the love of God which is in Christ Jesus. Not even 'neither virginity nor promiscuity' and all points between can separate you from this love. You are loved— without condition—beyond your wildest dreams already."[2]

My eyes filled with tears when I read Bessey's words. They were a balm in Gilead. I hadn't realized that the wounds of my premarital sexual activity still smarted; by the time I read the essay, I'd been married more than a decade. But those wounds were deep. They resisted healing. And they were particularly raw during the first year of our marriage.

Benjamin isn't a controlling or jealous person. He would have accepted me for exactly who I was and what I had done—if I had let him. But I didn't. Although he had not been formed by the same Christian subculture as I had and didn't have the same misgivings about premarital sex, during our courtship I felt the need to protect myself and my story the only way I knew how. I fibbed. I fudged. I reshaped the rougher edges of my sexual history and revised a timeline or two to make myself look more wholesome. As the truth dribbled out, as the truth has a way of doing, Benjamin was livid. The falsehoods in question hadn't put his health at risk, thankfully, though falsehoods about sexual activity certainly can. It wasn't the string of boyfriends that momentarily turned me, in his eyes, into a cup of backwash. It was the lies. After it was all finally out, I was again naked and ashamed. Unlike when I was nineteen, however, Benjamin met my vulnerability with tenderness and forgiveness—not for what wasn't his to forgive, but for everything that was.

I was experiencing a first. It was the first time I had ever been *fully* naked, the first time I was stripped not only of clothing but also of conceit, of charm, of armor, of fear. And it was safe—*I* was safe—because I was in the arms of a husband who loved me.

In that moment of physical, spiritual, and emotional exposure, I caught a convincing glimpse of why one might argue that sex is best kept within the boundaries of marriage. I began to understand why God might even go so far as to issue a strongly worded edict prohibiting premarital sex, backed by the convicting presence of the Holy Spirit. It was only a fleeting glimpse, only a burgeoning understanding. I still wondered if the lingering shame I felt about my premarital sexual encounters had been instilled in me by a subculture that demands (especially from women) an arbitrarily defined purity.

And yet. The line in Sarah Bessey's essay that struck the deepest chord for me was this: "It's likely you would make different choices, if you knew then what you know now."

There it is again: *knowledge*.

I know now, and am known now, in ways that my immature adolescent self could never have accessed or understood. I wish to take Bessey's advice: "Don't make it more than it is, and don't make it less than it is." But "it" is *something*, and it's my responsibility to suss out precisely what that something is.

I know now, and am known now, in marriage.

A book I begrudgingly appreciate is *The Meaning of Marriage* by Timothy Keller. Keller is not my theological cup of tea. He embraces traditional gender roles and rejects same-sex marriage, and these points are not marginal to his arguments. They are central to his take on the whole institution of marriage. So while I longed to write him off on principle, I found myself nevertheless affirming a great deal of what I read, particularly his take on premarital sex.

> One of the reasons we believe in our culture that sex should always and only be the result of great passion is that so many people today have learned how to have sex outside of marriage, and this is a very different experience than having sex inside it. Outside of marriage, sex is accompanied by a desire to impress or entice someone. It is something like the thrill of the hunt. When you are seeking to draw in someone you don't know, it injects risk, uncertainty, and pressure to the lovemaking that quickens the heartbeat and stirs the emotions.[3]

Many will roll their eyes at this blanket statement. After all, according to Keller, he and his wife were virgins on their wedding night. What does he actually know about what it's like to have sex before marriage? Surely this is a reductive blanket assessment of casual or committed-but-not-married sex. There are no doubt a wide variety of ways to experience unmarried sex. But for me? Yeah. The shoe fits. I can see it now. My relationships with boyfriends were devoid of any true intimacy. Sure, on rare occasions the sex was great—but it was never truly good.

The contrast between unmarried and married sex is significant. The covenant of marriage—the vows to love now and forever—changes everything. It just *does*. In an infamous and controversial op-ed piece for the *New York Times*, conservative columnist David Brooks makes a case for marriage equality by advocating for the domesticating influence of marriage irrespective of sexual orientation. "Anybody who has several sexual partners in a year is committing spiritual suicide," he hyperbolizes. "He or she is ripping the veil from all that is private and delicate in oneself, and pulverizing it in an assembly line of selfish sensations. But marriage is the opposite. Marriage joins two people in a sacred bond. It demands that they make an exclusive commitment to each other and thereby takes two discrete individuals and turns them into kin."[4]

But maybe this isn't such a hyperbole at all. Again, Keller's words give voice to what I struggle to name. He writes of his early experiences of sexual expression with his lawfully wedded wife: "With sex, we were trying to be vulnerable to one another, to give each other the gift of barefaced rejoicing in one another, and to know the pleasure of giving one another pleasure."[5] *Yes*. This is what Sarah Jane experienced from the first time she disrobed in the presence of her husband. It took time for me to get to this place that these couples experienced from the first night of their honeymoons. I had to relearn sexuality: to extricate it from shame and to dispose of the self-protections I had needed when I engaged in physical intimacy without the security of marriage.

This was a slow process, not unlike grieving a loss. Much of it happened incrementally, with a couple of climaxes along the way. (See what I did there?) There was that one night, not long after our older daughter was born. I had healed from childbirth well enough to entertain the possibility of intercourse with my husband again. In the midst of our love-making, I was suddenly overcome with the obvious: we had made a *baby*. We had made a baby *by doing precisely what we were at that very moment doing again*, however gingerly. The beauty of this shocked me—shocked the shame right out of me. The sex felt so right in every way. No matter that we were very much in crisis, having had our world turned upside down by our beloved yet ever-squalling progeny. It was great. It was good.

I fatalistically fret that a renewed embrace of chastity before marriage is an unrealistic ideal; we live in a culture in which those gates are wide and irreversibly open. I'm very glad that people are no longer shunned for "shacking up." But in many circles, one is hard-pressed to find a couple that *doesn't* live together before marriage these days—if they ever get married at all. I completely infuriated a liberal Christian friend recently by telling her that I suspect I might actually believe that sex is for married people. She chafes against the establishment of behavioral norms, seeing them as a source of oppression—especially for women, who have historically shouldered the burden of the consequences for disregarding them. She thinks I am still gripping the unnaturally heavy baggage of my evangelical youth, that my negative evaluation of my premarital experimentation is the result of powerful cultural taboos. What about her unmarried yet committed friends that have been together for a decade—are they "living in sin"? Are they selfishly fulfilling their own desires, unable to access the sort of cleaving of flesh and union of souls available to properly married couples?

I don't know what to say to her. I don't know what to say to my own dear friends who lived together shamelessly and happily for more than a decade before they married. Theirs was, by all accounts and appearances, as stable and loving and committed a relationship as any marriage, including my own, and no doubt quite a bit more stable and loving and committed than many marriages. The same is true for dear friends who found unexpected joy and pleasure in a late-in-life romance; for a variety of practical reasons, marriage wasn't an option. I have neither grounds nor desire to judge them. I can say in theory that the covenant of marriage, the vows to love now and forever, changes everything—but I can't say it to *their* faces because when I witness their great love for one another, the words turn to dust in my mouth.

In an essay for the *Christian Century*, Gerald W. Schlabach contends that the oft-ignored Pauline teaching to marry rather than to burn is worth revisiting. "'To burn' may stand for all the ways that we human beings, left to ourselves, live only for ourselves, our own pleasures, and our own survival. By contrast, 'to marry' may signal the way that all of us (even those who do so in a vocation of lifelong celibacy) learn to bend our desires away from ourselves, become vulnerable to the desires of others, and bend toward the service of others. This is a good thing for all."[6] Schlabach complicates easy notions about marriage; some who are technically married might still be "burning." Some who are not technically married may well be bending in ways that embody the grace and refuge of covenanted love. All of this is to say that while I long to uphold a sexual ethic of chastity for unmarried Christians, I don't know how to do this without acknowledging that there may well be exceptions to the ideal—or, at the very least, *complications* to the ideal.

I don't know how to encourage my parishioners—let alone my own children—to consider saving certain intimacies for the wedding night without descending into the same sort of supercilious finger-wagging that contributed to the calcification of my shame. And then there's the hypocrisy angle; how do I preach abstinence when I myself failed to abstain? *Do as I say, not as I did.* But as Paul cautioned, "Every other sin a person commits is outside the body, but the sexually immoral person sins against his own body" (1 Corinthians 6:18 ESV). I know this firsthand. So perhaps I hold up my pain: all that fooling around before marriage ever did was give me a world of hurt. But I can't hold up my pain without also lifting high my joy: all that fooling around *within* marriage ever did was give me a world of healing.

5

NEEDING
THE VOWS

On our thirteenth anniversary, Benjamin and I were back in northeast Ohio, visiting family and immersing ourselves in unchecked nostalgia. There is nothing quite like returning to a place once called home—a place where we made our best and our worst choices, both of which have utterly shaped our lives.

We celebrated at the Corner Cup, a new local coffee shop, our favorite old café having closed its doors not long after we moved away. Over coffee and cranberry scones, we talked about our relationship. Or rather, I talked about our relationship. I mused aloud that I didn't think we would have gotten married if we had decided to wait.

Benjamin protested. "Don't say that," he said. I tried to explain myself, saying that if we'd postponed our engagement to give ourselves more than three months as a couple before we made the big commitment, we would have fought enough to convince ourselves we were better apart, and we wouldn't have gotten married. He protested again. "Stop saying that."

I tried a third time, this time intending to make it crystal clear that I was *very* glad we had done what we did, that we needed to go through all that early trauma within the covenant of marriage or else we would have given up. But he interrupted before I could finish. He could not bear to hear me say it again. He could not bear to imagine that it all might not have been.

I don't want to imagine it either, but I needed to say it. Apparently I needed to say it three times: marriage was the only way for us to be *us*.

The summer we married, we were counselors at a day camp for children with developmental disabilities. I'd gotten the job first, but when the director mentioned she was short on male counselors, Benjamin applied—with the condition that he have a chance to take a nap between the end of his night shift at the group home and the start of his day at camp. The camp administrators were so relieved to have him they didn't mind that he turned up bleary-eyed at ten o'clock every morning, and Benjamin was so relieved to make some more money he didn't mind turning up bleary-eyed at ten o'clock every morning.

Every morning I anxiously awaited the sound of his Ford pickup truck on the gravel road. I wanted to be around him in general, but more to the point, I wanted him around at camp. He was good with the kids, conscientious, trustworthy.

I could depend on him in a way I couldn't depend on our other coworkers.

You can't really take an extended vacation from a summer job—especially with finances like ours—so we took an unpaid day off the Friday before our wedding and reported back to camp the Monday after. It was so surreal to show up as newly minted spouses that I wondered if the campers and counselors believed we actually had done this momentous thing during our brief absence.

In the afternoons, the campers went swimming in Silver Lake. I'd previously worked as a waterfront lifeguard at another camp, and so here I agonized over the comparatively lax safety measures we followed. No safety checks, no compulsive counting of campers. A solitary bored lifeguard sat slumped in a lawn chair on the beach. I managed my worry by positioning myself right in the midst of the swimmers, glancing away from the kids in the water only to give the stink eye to the counselors who chatted and laughed on the shore.

A few days after our wedding, I was trailing after a particularly poor swimmer when a peculiar chill came over me. It was a cloudless afternoon and the lake was warm from weeks of summer heat, yet my skin was suddenly peppered with goosebumps. I waded back to shore and told the director I'd taken ill. Somehow I drove myself back to our second-floor walk-up. By the time Benjamin returned I was groaning on the couch, delirious with fever.

Benjamin made himself dinner and fell asleep on the futon in our bedroom. I woke up in the middle of the night confused, sweaty, and vaguely convinced I was dying. Benjamin had already left for his job at the group home. There was nothing in the house save for a few pieces of stale wedding cake. I needed juice, chicken noodle soup, and something to quell my pounding headache and chip away at my persistent fever. More than anything, I needed someone to take care of me. I curled up on the couch and waited for Benjamin to come home.

When he did, he was exhausted. I knew he couldn't call off work, and I knew he needed to sleep. But in the moments he was around, I craved some attention and at least a whiff of pity. Instead, he made a wide berth around my sick bed. I was bereft. I called my parents, who snapped into action immediately. My mother picked me up and took me home—to their home, to the home that was no longer my home since I had a new home. She tried to nurse me back to health and, when that failed, took me to the doctor to get the chest X-rays that confirmed that I had a raging and inexplicable case of mid-summer pneumonia.

Benjamin visited me at my parents' house in between a shift at the group home and the camp. Fairly or not, I was furious with him. He, not my mother, was supposed to be the one taking care of me. I was convinced that he didn't really believe I was sick, but also afraid he did believe it but somehow didn't care enough to be my caregiver. I made sure to hack extra piteously when he said goodbye.

Still sick and still sulky, I had just moved back to our apartment when we received word that Benjamin's paternal grandfather had passed away. We needed to travel to Joliet, Illinois, for the funeral, immediately. Given the brevity of our courtship and engagement, I hadn't yet been introduced to much more than his immediate family, and virtually none of the relatives on his father's side.

And so it came to pass that, miserable from pneumonia and before most newlyweds have even returned from their honeymooning, I met the whole extended Pershey family as they grieved the loss of their patriarch. *Welcome to married life.*

We had vowed to one another, just days before, to "have and to hold" in good times and bad. It's easy to romanticize what this might look like. You imagine lovers laughing over chipped thrift-store bowls filled with ramen noodles. You imagine a shoulder to cry on in your darkest hour. You imagine squeezing some bravery into the hand of your beloved as he approaches the casket containing the lifeless body of the grandfather he dearly loved.

And you get those things. But you also get angrily pointed fingers when the too-steep credit card bill arrives in the mail. You get ugly fights during which you can't comfortably cry on one another's shoulders because you are the ones making one another cry; you are the ones pushing one another off the ledge into the valley of the shadow of death. You get a panic attack in the motel room in Joliet hours after the family-only graveside service because you realize you really didn't have a clue what you were getting into and you have two weeks to recover normal lung capacity and pack up the pickup for the cross-country move to California with this relative stranger who is now your lawfully married husband.

The first two weeks of our marriage were a microcosm of the first few years of our marriage. In a word: difficult. Not without moments of great joy. But if I only get a single word, the word is *difficult.*

But getting married makes it really hard to leave. Not impossible, obviously. The rise of no-fault divorce and the fact that ending a marriage no longer guarantees social and economic ruin means that virtually any marriage is eligible for termination. Before July 13, we could have simply broken up. The consequences would have been negligible: loss of face and a few deposits. After July 13, we couldn't escape one another without the involvement of lawyers, the signing of divorce papers, the breaking of a sacred covenant.

Which is not to say that I wanted to leave. Even as my panic attacks became a regular occurrence, I didn't chant, between hyperventilated breaths, "I wish I hadn't done this." I knew we had taken an extraordinary risk when we licked the envelopes of the wedding invitations and signed our names on the marriage license application. I knew Benjamin was a newly sober alcoholic and that I tended toward anxiety and low-level depression, especially in times of great change. We were both moody and selfish and remarkably lacking in self-awareness—hardly ideal grounds for domestic serenity. That our early married days were difficult—and not merely circumstantially difficult, what with the pneumonia and the death in the family and the relocation, but relationally difficult—really should have been no surprise.

We needed the vows to carry us through the moments of rage. We needed the public commitment to carry us through the exchanges of indignation. We needed the county-issued, clergy-signed marriage certificate to carry us through pneumonia and mourning and anxiety and seminary and debt and job interviews and pregnancy and postpartum depression *and you get the picture*. We needed to be one flesh—husband

and wife—to get through the day, let alone the years. Love alone wouldn't have been enough.

Dietrich Bonhoeffer wrote a wedding homily for his niece and her fiancé from the cell in which he was imprisoned by the Third Reich. In the homily, the German pastor and theologian writes, "God makes your marriage indissoluble, and protects it from every internal and external danger. . . . Free from all the anxiety that is always inherent in love, you may now with certainty and full of confidence say to each other: we can never lose each other; through God's will we belong to each other until death."[1]

The notion of marital indissolubility is viewed with suspicion these days; while most couples intend to stay married for the long haul and prenuptial agreements are still fairly rare, there seems to be broad consensus within both church and culture that divorce is a reasonable dissolvent for the purportedly indissoluble.

Within some churches, anyway. Roman Catholic doctrine rejects divorce; Catholics whose marriages have ended must endure an annulment process in which their marriages are declared invalid from the start (often for the presence of a "grave defect of discretion of judgment concerning the essential matrimonial rights"[2]). Without an annulment, divorced Catholics are unwelcome to receive Holy Communion. I struggle with this. I don't want people who seek divorce to be met with judgment, condemnation, gossip, or excommunication—and to be sure, these consequences are meted out in all sorts of communities, and are hardly limited to the Roman Catholic context. I believe that divorce must be a safe, affordable, and readily available option, not merely for those cases

of abuse in which it is profoundly unethical to encourage
or coerce an endangered spouse to stay. The rise of no-fault
divorce has been connected to the decrease in the suicide rate,
particularly among women; the presence of a way out saves
lives.[3]

However, the possibility of divorce as an option means
there is an enormous, blinking, neon asterisk at the end
of Bonhoeffer's assurance, and at the end of such biblical
teachings as Matthew 19:6. "So they are no longer two, but
one flesh. Therefore what God has joined together, let no
one separate."*

*Unless . . . well. Things happen.

I wonder if the mere presence of that asterisk is enough
to tear asunder marriages that could otherwise be redeemed.
I wonder this, but I don't know what to do with my wondering. Who gets to judge whether a marriage is worth the
effort to salvage? Who has the right to determine whether
a divorce is justifiable? Who decides when a couple has
fought the good fight and should just reconcile themselves to
their irreconcilability?

As I think through these thorny issues, I keep circling back
to these questions of authority. The lines of authority used to
be so much clearer in the premodern and modern eras. Not
that this was necessarily a good thing. I don't want to return
to a world in which women were disenfranchised and subju-
gated and one's life was at the mercy of institutional, social,
and parental powers. I want autonomy, and agency, and the
power to do what I have discerned is right—and I want this
for each individual.

Still, unbridled individualism has its downsides. The unbridled individual cannot, for instance, truly surrender to a sacrament of marriage that asks her to become one with another human being. Marriage is a bridling. The vows themselves establish profound limitations on individual freedom. You cannot do anything you please if the thing you please trespasses against the promises you made. You become subject to the other. Andrew J. Cherlin, sociologist and author of *The Marriage-Go-Round*, confirms my suspicions. His book is grounded in the argument that "in American culture, marriage and individualism form a contradictory pair of models."[4] We value marriage—*Till death do we part*. We value individualism—*I'm just not happy anymore*. And we just sort of look away when the value we place on marriage contradicts the value we place on personal satisfaction. Some southern states have established laws in which couples can opt for a "covenant" marriage; these distinct licenses require premarital counseling and limit how quickly and easily a couple can divorce. Cherlin notes that very few couples choose to accept the restrictions of covenant marriage. Americans "value the stability and security of marriage, but they tend to believe that individuals who are unhappy with their marriages should be allowed to end them. What Americans want, in other words, is for everyone else to have a covenant marriage."[5] Touché, Professor Cherlin. Touché.

For me—for us—I want to flick the asterisk away. I want union. I want there to be no seams in this garment revealing where God knit us together into one flesh. I want covenant marriage, spiritually if not legally.

I want forever.

6

HOMEWARD CRAWL

There's a country song that, like many country songs, seems designed to singlehandedly build the coffers of Kleenex shareholders. It's a total tear-jerker, if you happen to be the kind of person who is susceptible to that sort of thing.

A father croons about his daughter who has left home without a trace, presumably in a fit of angry, late adolescent wanderlust. She certainly hasn't left for law school; the subtext is she's gone wild, maybe even drinkin' and druggin' and befriending strange men. Just in case she calls, her father leaves a message on his answering machine telling her how much he loves her and welcoming her back home again. The message of welcome becomes the song's refrain. By the end of the song you know the wayward daughter returns to her forgiving father; she leaves a conveniently rhyming message that alerts him to her impending homecoming. It's hokey, sappy, and more than a little emotionally manipulative, but I've never once managed to listen to it without tearing up. As a Christian, I can't help but recognize that it is a twangy retelling of the parable of the prodigal son.

I encountered the same parable several years ago in a breathtakingly beautiful sculpture that is installed in one of the chapels on the campus of the National Cathedral in Washington, D.C. With just a cursory glance, it appears to be a crucifix. Only it is not. There is indeed a figure of a man affixed to the cross. His arms are not raised for crucifixion, however, but are embracing the figure of a second man. A father and his son, joined in a reconciling embrace. The sculptor, Gurdon Brewster, explains, "Welcome home is at the heart of our spiritual life. This sculpture is more than the father welcoming home the prodigal son. It is also the mother and daughter, the son and the mother, two friends long apart, two people who love each other, as well as the lonely, the lost, the rejected and the guilty finding God's absolute acceptance in the heart of the cross."[1] I was in the chapel for a worship service, of which I recall precisely nothing because I was so transfixed by the sculpture behind the preacher.

I've been pondering what the well-worn parable might look like if it were a story of betrayal not by a prodigal son but by a prodigal spouse. It isn't a big stretch, really, to tinker with the roles and relationships in this little allegory. One of the prevailing images of God in the Christian faith is that God is our Father. But in the Hebrew Bible, one of the metaphors for the relationship between God and the Israelites is that of husband and wife, and the New Testament introduces the metaphor that the church is the bride of Christ.

When I think about the story from this perspective, I find myself having even more sympathy for the older brother. The son who was not a prodigal. The son who was faithful to his responsibilities. The son who stayed.

I imagine the figure hiding out during the celebratory party not as the indignant elder son but as the Wronged Wife. I imagine that the Prodigal Son is not the Prodigal Son at all but the Philandering Husband. I imagine that he darted away not from the family farm but from his marriage vows. Maybe it started off innocently enough, but like so many men and women before him, he did not check himself before he wrecked himself. And his marriage. The Prodigal Son saw the light only when he found himself reduced to eating swine feed. Maybe the Philandering Husband discovered he was still the same broken man even in the arms of another woman, that the novelty of illicit sex had not chased away his insecurities or made him any more capable of love and intimacy. If anything, the affair restored his reserves of self-hatred and sabotaged his ability to trust (let alone to be trusted). Or maybe he reveled in every minute of his tawdry adventure—the sex, the freedom, the fantasy come to life—and only realized his treachery and accessed his shame when the Other Woman slipped away before dawn, having left a note on the pillow stating the obvious: *It's over.*

So begins his reverse journey, the defeated homeward crawl. In this revised, nonstandard version, the father is still the Heavenly Father, letting the screen door bang as he races out to meet the repentant sinner. There he offers that reconciling embrace that has inspired country singers and sculptors and an innumerable host of sinners who have taken the risk of returning home.

But in this retelling, I imagine the Wronged Wife on the heels of the Heavenly Father, desperate to reach the Philandering Husband first. Not because she wants to welcome him home with a kiss and a casserole, but because she wants to give him a piece of her mind. This imagined scenario comes to life in Beyoncé's 2016 visual album, *Lemonade*—particularly through the song "Don't Hurt Yourself." She confronts an unfaithful spouse with unrestrained fury, flinging her wedding ring along with a warning: "If you try this s--- again, you're gonna lose your wife."[2] The first time I watched the video, I felt compelled to avert my eyes. Beholding such distress and rage is unnerving. Yet this is the power of *Lemonade*: Beyoncé demands witnesses to the pain of betrayal.

The reconciling embrace may well be breathtakingly beautiful, theologically speaking. The moral of the story is that God is scandalously forgiving, and that's great. But here's the thing: sometimes it can be hard to be joyful about all that scandalous forgiveness, and harder yet to join in and forgive. I believe in forgiveness, but I also believe that people who have been wronged need to establish boundaries and protect themselves. It isn't fair to put spiritualized pressure on someone to race to embrace the very person who has betrayed them. Neither is it right for forgiveness to simply pave the way for victims to be victimized again. I would be deeply concerned if a woman whose husband cheated on her left a voicemail begging him to come home—free and clear, no questions asked— as the father in the song pleaded to his daughter.

Not that I believe reconciliation is impossible. In an essay about *Lemonade* for *Think Christian*, Tamara Hill Murphy notes, "The couples who make it gloriously to the other side of pain to full reconciliation are the ones who are willing to enter the messy, painful stages of grief."[3] This is why Murphy lauds the album; by the end of the harrowing song cycle, Beyoncé implies she and her Philandering Husband are reconciled. Such reconciliation takes enormous work—facing uncomfortable truths, rebuilding broken trust, reestablishing healthy boundaries. Most couples need the assistance of a trained marriage counselor to walk with them on that journey. "Come home, no questions asked" is no more reconciliation than peace is the absence of tension.

Maybe the elder brother is hiding out in the field for a good reason: he isn't merely angry that his father forgave his brother and threw a party to celebrate his return. Maybe he's safeguarding himself from being betrayed again. Of course, the beautiful thing is that the Father comes to him, too, just as he raced out to meet the Prodigal.

I know that this is a story about forgiveness. As a responsible reader of the biblical narrative, I'm supposed to let the story be what the story wants to be. But what I really want to say is that we should probably talk a little more about honoring the promises we make. We should say that the Prodigal Son should not be such a selfish narcissist, and that husbands and wives should straight up not cheat on one another. I want to say that we should live in ways that do not leave our loved ones brokenhearted. And I think I can still say this, right? Just because God forgives the sins does not mean they are not sins.

Esther Perel, a therapist and the author of *Mating in Captivity: Unlocking Erotic Intelligence*, is one of a small but vocal minority of therapists who equivocate about the evils of infidelity. She freaks me out. It's one thing for an unrepentant womanizer to rationalize his string of seductions; it's another thing altogether for a credentialed counselor to propose, however implicitly, that affairs can be justified. In an article for *Psychotherapy Networker*, Perel writes:

> People stray for many reasons—tainted love, revenge, unfulfilled longings, and plain old lust. At times, an affair is a quest for intensity, a rebellion against the confines of matrimony. An illicit liaison can be catastrophic, but it can also be liberating, a source of strength, a healing. And frequently it's all these things at once. Some affairs are acts of resistance; others happen when we offer no resistance at all. Straying can sound an alarm for the marriage, signaling an urgent need to pay attention to what ails it. Or it can be the death knell that follows a relationship's last gasping breath.[4]

As I ponder these words in light of the reimagined parable of the Philandering Husband and Wronged Wife (which could, of course, just as readily be populated by the Philandering Wife and Wronged Husband), I can't help but contemplate how the most wretched of sinners seem to end up filled with the most amazing grace. Jesus did say healthy people do not need a doctor; he came to heal the sick. Stories of redemption and healing are glorious, worth telling and retelling. And so we're stuck with the paradox of celebrating the liberation and strength and healing that can emerge from crisis. But I reckon we must do this without justifying—let alone celebrating—the clandestine liaison that set off the crisis. Paul nailed it in his letter to the Romans: "Should we continue in sin in order that grace may abound? By no means! How can we who died to sin go on living in it?" (Romans 6:1-2).

There is a part of me that wants this parable to be entirely different. It's so human to thirst for the story in which the sinner is punished. We like our just desserts. Instead we get the story in which the sinner is loved and welcomed home. But this and all the parables are full of nuance, full of ethical questions and theological conundrums, full of saints who are never entirely good and villains who have hearts of gold. These stories are full of nuance—except when they are not. One thing in the Bible is not nuanced at all: the love of God. There's no nuance to God's love. There's no end to it. There's no fairness to it. We can't hide from it. We can't even satisfactorily reject it, because no matter what we do, God loves us. If you have betrayed your promises to another, God loves you. If you have been so betrayed you can't come in from the cold, God loves you. If you love God with all your heart and soul and mind and heart, God loves you. If you don't, God loves you. If you love your neighbor as yourself, God loves you. If you don't, God loves you.

In one of the interrelated plots of the terribly wonderful (or is it wonderfully terrible?) movie *Love, Actually*, Karen's husband, Harry, buys a necklace for another woman. Karen finds out. In an excruciating scene, she confronts Harry. "Would you wait around to find out if it's just a necklace, or if it's sex and a necklace, or if, worst of all, it's a necklace and love? Would you stay, knowing life would always be a little bit worse? Or would you cut and run?" The gravity of

Harry's unfaithfulness washes over him; he is deeply ashamed of himself. He tells his wife that he is a fool. "Yes," Karen responds. "But you've also made a fool out of me, and you've made the life I lead foolish too!" She has experienced an agonizing betrayal, and she cannot help but weigh the risk of forgiveness. I suspect this fictional character, if faced with Perel's claim that infidelity can be "healing" for a relationship, would laugh in her face. Stay or leave: after an infidelity of any degree, life would always be a little bit worse.

William S. Burroughs writes, "There is no intensity of love or feeling that does not involve the risk of crippling hurt. It is a duty to take this risk, to love and feel without defense or reserve."[5] This is the risk that God takes in loving us. Perhaps God alone can truly love without an ounce of defense or reservation, God alone can rush to meet the betrayer and the betrayed with equally open arms. But we love because God first loved us. We take risks because in forming us out of the dust of the earth and breathing life and spirit into our nostrils, God risked everything. We take risks because God risked everything to send Christ, our Holy Fool, whose foolishness is ever wiser than human wisdom.

We take risks—to love, to marry—and hope that we will not be made fools by the ones to whom we have entrusted ourselves. And, just as surely as we take risks, we *are* risks. The one who has entrusted himself to me is hoping I will not make a fool of him, either.

7

BLESSING UPON BLESSING

It was the kind of voicemail that gives a pastor pause. Allison didn't quite sound like she was in crisis, but as she requested a call back, I could tell that something was bothering her. After a day of phone tag, she finally caught me at home. By that time my concern and curiosity had escalated, so I set down my onion and chopping knife to take the call.

There was no crisis, but there was a conundrum. Close friends of Allison were getting married. They had asked her husband to be the best man in the wedding, and—in a far more surprising invitation—they asked Allison to officiate at the ceremony. She was honored. She'd accepted the invitation on the spot, assuming that there must be some sort of process in place for a person who is neither a judge nor a clergyperson to obtain credentials to perform weddings.

There is a process by which a person can quickly become a clergyperson, and therein lay the cause for Allison's profound discomfort. No one has invented a fast track to judicial authority, but thanks to the Universal Life Church, anyone who agrees to "do only that which is right" can get ordained. Online. After all, the ULC "wants you to pursue your spiritual beliefs without interference from any outside agency, including government or church authority."[1] Clergy—"real" clergy—are notoriously agitated by websites like the ULC and the countless esteemed colleagues they churn out. ("You will receive notification of your ordination status by email. Ordinations are conducted several times each week, so normally you will hear from us within a day or two."[2])

It's not exactly territorialism we pastors feel. We're still the ones signing the marriage licenses of our own parishioners; many of the weddings these "ordained ministers" officiate would otherwise have taken place at courthouses. And while the reaction may be about pride, it's an understandable pride. A seminary-trained pastor—who faithfully endured her denomination's ordination process, who dutifully pursues the required continuing education requirements, who walked the bride and groom through a thoughtful premarital counseling process, and who prayerfully prepared a creative and meaningful wedding liturgy for the day—reported that she was recently asked at a wedding reception if she'd gotten ordained online. *As if!* Clergy are generalists, but weddings are one of our few specialized functions. Surely we are not entirely replaceable.

Allison felt extremely uncomfortable about the prospect of a ULC ordination. This was, I'll admit, a comfort to my ego and music to my ears. She explained that she had a deep respect for the office of the clergy. Reducing the ordination process to an order form, credit card, and printable certificate seemed to her like more than a cheapening of the vocation; it was a mockery of it. What's more, Allison is an adult convert to the United Church of Christ. Her own sense of religious identity would be compromised by the ruse of joining the ULC as a so-called religious leader. And yet it was such an honor to be asked by her friends that she couldn't bear the thought of calling them back to tell them she had changed her mind.

I suggested that she might ask her friends to have a private legal ceremony with a judge, after which she could preside over a public blessing and exchange of vows that subtly excluded legalities. This wasn't an unprecedented possibility. For various reasons, I have done such services; sometimes the couple can't wait until the wedding to proceed with the legal marriage. To be sure, many pastors celebrated commitment ceremonies without legal standing in the years before same-sex couples were granted access to marriage. Allison agreed that this could be a solution. Then she trailed off, her ambivalence apparent.

I realized at that moment that Allison wasn't looking for my help in finding a way out of doing what her friends were asking. What she wanted—even if she did not yet know it— was my blessing. Not my permission, not my acquiescence. My blessing.

I often underestimate the inherent authority that I have as a member of the clergy. Yes, I preach and baptize and consecrate, but as a pastor in a tradition with congregational polity, I rarely have a vote. Whatever pastoral authority I do possess, I don't wave around for the world or my parish to see. So the question I proceeded to ask did not come naturally to me. In fact, I felt a bit like I was impersonating the pope. I haltingly asked Allison if she would like me to grant her my blessing. Her answer was swift and relieved: yes.

I offered to help Allison think through the wedding liturgy, and she gratefully accepted. When we met several weeks later, our conversation touched on a constellation of related issues as well. We considered the causes and ramifications of the growing trend of couples enlisting friends or family to perform wedding ceremonies. We talked about the role of the church in a post-Christendom society. We lamented some of the ways marriage has been and is being transformed, and we celebrated others. We noted the peculiar custom of vesting legal power in otherwise strictly parochial authorities. I tried to assuage Allison's lingering guilt about having sent off for her ordination papers by reminding her that even American Marriage Ministries—a less polemical alternative to the Universal Life Church, founded by actual religious professionals—must call itself a church and issue ordinations, because that is what most states require.

But we didn't just talk religion and politics and culture. We also talked about the role of the church and marriage in our own lives. I was privileged, as I so often am in my work as a congregational minister, to hear Allison's story. It ended up being one of the most enjoyable and meaningful conversations I've shared with a parishioner. Most importantly, we prayed together. I asked God's blessing upon Allison's blessing of the marriage.

Not long after the newlyweds departed for their honeymoon, Allison sent me a note detailing her foray into my
world. I laughed at the classic clergywoman moment she
experienced when a sound expert was undone by the unlucky
jigsaw of the lapel microphone and Allison's lapel-less dress.
I cringed knowingly at her minor mistake of forgetting to
instruct the wedding guests to be seated, having made the
same mistake during my first wedding. I nodded as she marveled at the honor of it all—being a part of such a momentous
moment, not only for the bride and groom but also for the
community that gathered to bear witness and pledge support.

And finally, I rejoiced that officiating at this wedding had
the same effect on Allison as officiating at weddings invariably has on me. "Is this selfish?" she wondered. "One of the
greatest benefits of this experience is that it brought Dave and
me together in such a meaningful way," she said, referring to
her husband. "He helped me write and proofread the ceremony, and in so doing we found ourselves having many long
conversations about what love is, why we value our marriage, what we admire about other relationships, and how we
can support marriage. And we talked about the strengths and
weaknesses of our own marriage. I pulled out our own vows
and letters we wrote when we were engaged. Lovely. It was
just a lovely moment in our marriage."

I remain ambivalent about the rise of the nonprofessional
wedding officiant and the sidelining of the clergy. As the culture shifts away from institutions, it follows that it would
also shift away from institutional authorities. Should someone dare ask me at a wedding reception if I obtained my credentials online, I would have to concentrate very hard on not

kicking that person in the shins. I believe that what clergy offer—spiritual guidance, pastoral care, accountability to an imperfect but holy church—is valuable.

Yet even though I didn't perform this particular wedding ceremony, I did manage to offer those same gifts to Allison. She gladly received them and passed them on, in a sort of newfangled priesthood of all believers.

Her thank-you note to me included this William Wordsworth quote: "All that we behold is full of blessings." Inside, she wrote, "Thank you for beholding, providing, sharing, and helping me participate in blessings." I could say the same to her.

8

ALL THE MIRACLES

We celebrated our tenth anniversary shortly before we celebrated Ben's eleventh year of sobriety. When we toasted our family at a funky beachside restaurant on Lake Michigan, there was pop in his glass and beer in mine. We didn't talk much that night. It's usually hard for me to sit quietly. Benjamin is far more reserved than I am, far more content to just *be*. I have tried and failed on countless occasions to start a date night conversation with him by asking what he's thinking about; surely someday I will accept that this ploy will never work. But that night in Door County, even my spirit was still. We were toasting miracles—hoped for, worked for, nevertheless unforeseen.

During his early twenties, Benjamin had tried and failed to get sober time and time again. Almost as soon as he started drinking, it became clear he was a problem drinker. He wasn't a happy drunk. He was a sullen, stupid, intolerable drunk. Even though he has made amends wherever possible for the things he did during his drinking years, he still harbors regret for the person he became under the influence. He still feels guilty for the people he hurt under the influence. When we first met he was living in a halfway house, from which he was unceremoniously booted when he broke the rules by turning up one night intoxicated. At one point he managed to string together eleven dry months, but invariably, his urge to drink would suffocate his willpower to abstain. Until I came along. He guzzled his last pint of beer at a John Mellencamp concert the night before we went on our first date.

I had just turned twenty-one and was still enjoying the novelty of being able to legally drink alcohol. I was looking forward to figuring out what kind of wine I liked. I suspected I would be a rosé girl, somewhere between the classiness of white wine and the weight of red. But with Benjamin as my date, my boyfriend, my fiancé, my husband—I couldn't do something so dangerous and silly as *drink*. So I didn't. And, remarkably, he didn't either.

Our relationship and Benjamin's sobriety were bound together, at times perhaps unhealthily so. Once I shared something I'd written about this part of our relationship during a writing workshop, and the first workshop partici-pant to respond didn't address my writing but my codepen-dency. "Get thee to Al-Anon," she exhaled. I was irritated, but mostly because she was right. I could support Ben in his sobriety, but I could not do it for him.

Starting to drink alcohol again seemed like a ridiculous risk: my husband's sobriety for a craft beer? At the same time, it felt powerful and freeing and healthy. I was not trading my husband's sobriety for a fleeting pleasure; his sobriety had long since been extricated from mine. He was stronger—so much stronger—and most importantly, he had relearned how to walk the steps that have been a life-saving grace for so many formerly stumbling drunks. After a great deal of conversation, prayer, and consultation with our marriage counselor, we decided it was safe for me to drink again, after eight years of prohibition. It was precisely that process that helped us rediscover that we are, in fact, two separate people.

I don't regret my eight years of not drinking. Benjamin needed me to do it. He needed a kitchen that wasn't stocked with Blue Moon and a wife whose kiss did not convey a whiff of gin and tonic. He needed me to help carry the burden of his sobriety in every way I could. It was a small sacrifice, an act of solidarity, a form of communion by abstention. And then, eventually, he didn't need me to do it anymore. Or, perhaps, he sacrificed his need for me not to drink. So often this is what marriage is: a dance of reciprocal sacrifice and mutual compromise.

I drank: happily, and enjoying the fruits of the vine and adulthood from the cup I had expected would continue to pass me by.

One night while Ben was at his weekly recovery meeting, I settled onto the couch with a book of poetry and a new winter porter. I am unsurprisingly nerdy about my drinking. I want to tour breweries, learn all I can about the fermentation process, and drink what the connoisseurs declare sublime. I was curious about the porter, and took to the Internet to find more information. The brewery referred to it as *nourishing*.

I found this moving and wonderfully familiar. The same drink that is poison to my husband is nourishing to me. The same drink that could have killed my beloved Benjamin gives me joy.

I used to despise the story of Jesus turning water into wine. I was incensed that the church where we were married covered our bulletin with their standard wedding clip art, which featured Jesus at the wedding in Cana. It felt like insult added to injury, as the priest had decreed that we could not include communion during our wedding service if we were unwilling to have the chalice filled with sacramental wine instead of nonalcoholic grape juice. The story of Jesus supplying the already intoxicated wedding guests with more wine struck me as an unnecessary betrayal of my husband.

But on the shores of Lake Michigan that night, I rejoiced in all the miracles: The first sign of the reign of Jesus. The first decade of our marriage. Ben's whiskey turned into Coca-Cola. My water turned into ale.

Cheers—and thanks be to God.

9

LONG
OBEDIENCE

It is strange to think of a particular person as the person with whom I did not have an affair. There are, in fact, many people with whom I have not had an affair. Billions. I have never slept with the mailman, or kissed my ex-boyfriend, or flirted with a stranger (at least not on purpose—sometimes I can't contain my natural charm). Since I've never been unfaithful to my husband, there are a remarkable number of people with whom I have not committed adultery.

And yet there is one man I cannot help but think of as the man with whom I did not cheat on Benjamin. We had no improper physical contact, no inappropriately intimate conversations. I don't even know if the attraction was mutual. There was, however, temptation. I felt desire. And when it comes to marriage, temptation and desire are nearly as shameful as actually giving in. Just ask Jimmy Carter, who infamously confessed to *Playboy* magazine, "I've looked on a lot of women with lust. I've committed adultery in my heart many times."[1] Carter's words made the nation cringe. But Jesus was the first to equate lust with adultery of the heart.

It doesn't seem fair. When my jeans start to fit too snugly, I track my diet. I don't have to tally up the slice of German chocolate cake I didn't eat. It doesn't matter how hungry I am, how badly I long to devour that frosting with a spoon and let it dissolve on my tongue until only flakes of sweet coconut remain. I could look up recipes for German chocolate cake in my ridiculously large library of cookbooks. I could buy all the ingredients at the grocery store after work. I could bake the damn cake, but so long as a single morsel doesn't pass through my lips, I haven't done anything worth reporting to my food diary.

Having never actually had an affair, I'm no expert. But I reckon this is how it goes: You think you can have your cake without eating it, too. Invariably, you give in and indulge. And that's fine if the cake is just cake; you just won't be able to zip your trousers tomorrow. But if the cake is a handy metaphor for the man to whom you are not married—well, congratulations. You've committed adultery. Even if you never unzip your trousers, you've managed to carry on a doozy of an emotional affair. You've committed adultery in your heart.

When I realized that I had feelings for this man, I was shocked. I almost didn't recognize the crush for what it was, it had been such a long time since I'd had one. I knew that when I piled my lunch onto my tray and scanned the cafeteria for a place to sit, I was looking for him, eager for another soulful, meandering conversation. I knew that when

I decided which of the conference events I would attend and which ones I would skip, I hesitated to state my intentions until I'd heard his, and that, coincidentally enough, I always wanted to do the same things.

But it wasn't until Thursday afternoon that the crush became crushingly clear to me. We were sitting side by side in the plenary hall, listening to an author read rather monotonously from her latest book. We both shifted in our seats at precisely the same moment, uncrossing and recrossing our legs in a strange synchronicity. It was then I noticed it for the first time: the sense that we were inhabiting the same sphere of energy. It was as though chemicals in my body were responding, of their own volition, to chemicals in his. *Oh, dear*, I thought. *This isn't good*. And yet, if I am altogether honest with myself, I also thought the inverse. *This is so good*. It was disorienting, terrifying, the slightest bit exhilarating—like being on a roller coaster but knowing full well that upon hitting the last soaring loop-the-loop, the car will derail and you will plunge to your death. My internal alarms all tripped at once, clanging an overwhelming and persuasive warning. *Danger, danger.*

Danger, even though it wasn't primarily a physical attraction. If he had been an Adonis with a middling personality, I would have joked with my husband about my exceedingly hot new friend, just as he's been known to wink at me as he volunteers to take our kids to their gorgeous pediatrician. Rather, this man was brilliant and funny and kind and . . . well, I'm not here to drool over the cake.

The last night of the conference I still felt the maddening chemistry dancing between us. During a break in activities, I saw him standing near the entrance to the dormitories, alone. He waved. I wondered if this was an invitation or a figment of my overactive imagination. I waved back and returned to my room by way of the back stairwell, rehearsing the many reasons I would not act upon my mutinous desires. Most of the reasons had a name and a face.

A few hours later, during the closing reception, we sat together on a sofa, surrounded by other new friends. I had a very early shuttle to catch, so after a single nightcap I began making my farewells. I saved him for last, a gesture I hoped was merely an acknowledgment that we had found in one another kindred spirits. Even as I leaned in for a chaste hug, though, I caught one of our friends looking at us curiously. I could see a question in his eyes—suspicion. Perhaps the chemistry I perceived was perceivable by others; perhaps my behavior had given me away.

I turned and walked out of the reception hall, stopping just beyond the door, where I could stand for a moment unseen. In the moment our bodies had touched in that farewell embrace, it was as though the amorphous chemistry had become electrified, almost tangible. I wanted him almost as fiercely as I wanted to run from him. I wanted him to walk out of the party and find me standing there. But at the same time I felt myself yanked homeward, as if my wedding ring were miraculously, magnetically attracted to Benjamin's wedding ring across the gaping chasm of a thousand miles, across the undeniable slump in our marital joy.

I returned to my room and locked the door, grateful for the decisive click of the deadbolt. I Skyped Benjamin immediately. He answered his cell phone, agitated. After a week of being the sole parent on duty for feeding, clothing, and keeping our young children alive, he was tired and cranky. Thanks to a thunderstorm that had rumbled through the steamy Midwest, knocking out the electricity in its path, he was also uncomfortably hot. Without the lights on, the picture quality of the video was grainy. As we talked, he fixed his gaze out our bedroom window to our neighbors' house across the street, where police cars and fire trucks had assembled when a lightning bolt ignited a quick-burning fire on the pole near their house. The angle of the camera had me looking up his nose. I tried to act normal. I listened to the story, and calmly reminded him of my flight information, and told him I couldn't wait to see him the next day. I wondered if he could detect anything weird in my voice as we said goodnight, and again when he and the girls picked me up at the airport not a full twelve hours later.

Within the week, I did the only thing I could fathom: I told Benjamin everything. Even though there wasn't much to tell—oh, how profoundly glad I was to go to him with a clean conscience!—the conversation was risky. Would it wound him to know that his wife, though delivered from temptation, had experienced it? Yes, it did. But it was a hurt he could sustain, because he understood that at the root of what I was telling him was that I was trustworthy. I had been tested and proven faithful.

As we pondered the nuances of fidelity, a curious thing happened: our love for and attraction to each other deepened. Benjamin trusted me to nurture the new friendship, which I did with considerable caution and reserve, and which was further subdued by sheer geographical distance. I established

the boundaries that would govern my platonic relationship
with this man to whom I am not married, and in so doing, I
rediscovered the intrigue of my delightfully unbounded relationship with the man to whom I am. There is yet more for
us to know of each other, physically, spiritually, emotionally.
And as husband and wife we have the incredible freedom
to explore each other without hesitation or shame. There is
nothing to stop us from growing ever more intimate. Don't
believe anyone who says otherwise: fidelity can be sexy.
Very sexy.

In the time since I was delivered from temptation, I've
encountered countless stories of infidelity. They are everywhere; they always have been. They are featured in movies
and advice columns, tabloid glossies and institutional gloss-
overs. I receive these stories just a hair differently nowadays.
You would think I'd be more understanding, having stood
at such a precipice myself. I'm not. If anything, I'm more
inclined to indignation. *I walked away; why couldn't you?* I
fumed the last time a pastor publicly confessed to adultery.
(Why is so much worse when clergy cheat? Is it because we
generally have access to mental health resources and sys-
tems of accountability? Is it because we have an even greater
obligation to honor the covenants we make? Or maybe it is
because, as ambassadors of Christ and students of the Bible,
stepping out is just a royally hypocritical thing to do.)

My spiritual director reminded me of the story of the
woman caught in adultery. She more than reminded me, in
fact. She led me through a rich and insightful visualization
of the scene from the gospel of John. The adulterer's accusers
are ready to stone her in accordance with law and custom.

The scribes and Pharisees seize the opportunity to try to trick Jesus, cornering him between the rocks of cruelty and the hard place of heresy. As I prayerfully pictured the story, I imagined I held a cobblestone as round as a baseball. I forced myself to look at the disgraced pastor, huddled in shame and quaking with fear. Jesus, in a particularly brilliant subversion of the narrative, encourages anyone without sin to throw the first stone. It is as though the accused is protected by a shield of mirrors; each accuser is faced by his or her own reflection. I saw the truth of myself: the ugliness of my unrighteous anger, the content of my illicit desires, the depth of my own sin. Jesus would not command me to do it. I had to say the words to myself: *Put the rock down.* This became my mantra, particularly as the gossip mills swirled by, daring me to lob verbal pebbles at the pastor's reputation. *Put the rock down. Put it down, put it down.*

Though I marvel at the wisdom of Jesus in this story, I am reluctant to receive his grace. The Pharisee in me feels cheated of an opportunity to make a sinner pay, though the sinner in me knows that if I were on the other side of the rocks, I'd be awfully glad for the intervention. And, to be sure, I *am* the sinner, guilty as charged for my own misdeeds and totally at the mercy of a forgiving God. I am sent on my way with the same admonition to "go and sin no more."

I still think it's critical to recall the exceptional significance of fidelity in the biblical tradition, without resorting to hypocrisy or contempt. The prohibition against adultery is, after all, written in stone. Literally. And infidelity in marriage is intimately related to infidelity to God—because each is a covenant relationship. A covenant is an agreement not unlike a contract, save for one minor detail: it's completely unlike a contract. Contracts are conditional, limited, and generally entered into for reasons of self-interest. They are legal documents that can be used against you if you violate their terms. Covenants aren't legal, but they are sacred. They can be established between equals, such as two people, or unequals, such as God and God's people. And they are unconditional: if one party fails to follow through, the covenant *remains in place*. There's no statute of limitations. You cannot renegotiate terms. A contract is to a covenant as ink is to blood.

The first covenant is initiated by God after the flood. God promises never to do such a thing again. Noah, for his part, is supposed to refrain from mixing meat and blood, and to get cracking on the baby-making. The first covenant is sealed with a rainbow—which, along with all the zebra and turtle and rabbit pairs, explains why this violent, disturbing tale is often deemed appropriate for toddlers. A series of covenants follows, by which God identifies, blesses, and sets the chosen people apart. They come with steep and often bewildering expectations—have you *read* Leviticus?—but are always rooted in relationship. God is undeniably smitten with the descendants of Abraham. God wants this one to last, you know? As Jeremiah puts it, "They shall be my people, and I will be their God" (Jeremiah 32:38).

The amazing—and painful—thing is that by the time Jeremiah passes along this beautiful word of the Lord, God's beloved people have been totally and repeatedly screwing up for ages. They sin, and sin, and sin some more. And with a covenant in place, a sin isn't merely a violation of the law. It's a betrayal of the relationship; it's personal. The Israelites are being unfaithful.

At the beginning of the book of Hosea, God says to the prophet, "Go, take for yourself a wife of whoredom and have children of whoredom, for the land commits great whoredom by forsaking the Lord" (Hosea 1:2). Yes, the prophetic allegory employs some gender dynamics that are a tiny bit problematic. But the language of Hosea, with its sheer ferocity, also conveys the ravaging consequences of unfaithfulness. One does not use the word *whoredom* thrice in one sentence if one is not in extreme emotional pain.

Despite marrying Hosea and bearing his children, Gomer wanders. She cheats on her husband. She is the prodigal wife, disregarding the covenant of marriage by committing adultery. At one point she sells herself into slavery. But even then, God tells Hosea to extend mercy to her yet again by buying her back. Hosea loves and forgives his "wife of whoredom." God loves and forgives God's spiritually promiscuous people who trample on the covenant that is supposed to bind them to God and to one another, over and over and over again. God is merciful to an agonizing degree.

Dear God, I don't want to be Gomer. I don't want my marriage to be like that. I want to honor all the covenants that govern my life: marriage, yes, but also baptism and ordination. I don't want to sin against the ones I love.

Sometimes I wonder why we are surprised that so many marriages end in discarded vows and broken covenants. Humans are, it would seem, highly susceptible to infidelity. Yet there are vows that are cherished and covenants that are kept, and the consequence of mutual fidelity is a life steeped in blessings.

Not long ago, my church celebrated the sixtieth anniversary of our beloved associate minister's ordination. With a great deal of pomp and circumstance, we sent him forth into his well-deserved retirement. There were trumpets and breathtaking handmade gifts and original songs (twenty new verses to "For the Beauty of the Earth," each praising God for the various, sundry, and abundant gifts of Paul and his wife; no, we didn't sing them all, but we sang a whole lot). Paul preached his final sermon, "A Last and Lasting Word," which pointed not to his words but to the enduring Word of God. Then the congregation stood and applauded until our palms stung.

I feel extremely lucky to have served alongside Paul during the last years of his ministry. He is an old-school pastor in all the best ways, a modern mystic, and a wildly funny jokester. But what strikes me as most remarkable is his fidelity, what Eugene H. Peterson would call his "long obedience in the same direction." Paul has spent his entire life fulfilling the ordination vows he made when he was twenty-five, as well as the marriage vows he exchanged with his wife three years before that. His life is a brilliant, shining example of the beauty of covenant. Whenever a community celebrates a big anniversary—of a wedding or an ordination, and others, I'm sure—it is a lovely reminder that the grandiose promises one makes in one's youth can bear out, and bear fruit.

A "long obedience in the same direction" has its stretches marked by the strain of toil and the fret of care, but it also has its glorious mountaintop vistas and the camaraderie of good company. And sometimes—if you so happen to land in a place that knows how to party—a three-piece band playing Dixieland jazz sets up shop outside the sanctuary to fete you as you make your way to the fellowship hall to greet hundreds of people who love you because you have loved them so very, very well. If you ask me, nothing says "Well done, good and faithful servant" like a tuba, a clarinet, and a banjo.

On our way out of the retirement party, after the gifts had been given and the tear-streaked cheeks had been kissed, I danced with my daughters by the bandstand while Benjamin shook his head and laughed. I pretended my daughters were goading me to dance, but it was really the other way around. I wanted to savor this moment that was not our moment but had graciously become one of the moments in my own joyfully covenanted life, my own long obedience in the same direction.

10

FOR THOSE WHO MEANT FOREVER

The sanctuary of the first church I pastored was bright and clean. The attic of the sanctuary of my first church was not bright and not clean. It was dusty and creepy and filled with debris from the congregation's spiritual and communal life. There you might find liturgical banners from the 1970s, wheelchairs from the 1980s, and bank statements from the 1990s.

I hated to venture up there and rarely did, but that day I had no choice: the kneeler traditionally used during wedding ceremonies was stored, unceremoniously, in the midst of the mess. It was too heavy and unwieldy to haul down two narrow flights of stairs by myself, so I enlisted Benjamin to meet me at church after work to help. It was our wedding anniversary, but our own celebration would have to wait until we had prepared for someone else's.

As we appraised the blond wood in the late afternoon light, it was clear that the thing needed a scrubbing before it could be put to use; it is generally considered bad form for a bride's ivory gown to be blackened by dust mid-ceremony. While Benjamin dragged it into the garden courtyard, I fetched a bucket, a bottle of Murphy Oil Soap, and a couple of rags from the custodial closet. We began the project of systematically removing the attic grime.

As we scrubbed, I began feeling a bit sorry for myself and for Benjamin. This unsexy moment did not fit into my visions of marriage or ministry. Just then, however, Benjamin said the sort of thing Benjamin says. "This feels very marital."

And suddenly there wasn't anything I'd rather do on our wedding anniversary than to scrub a wedding kneeler, together.

My pastoral role in weddings still makes me nervous, but I was especially skittish about the first few I officiated. People often assume that funerals would be harder on pastors than weddings, and in some ways they are. But people don't spend years dreaming and months planning every single detail of a funeral, hoping that it will be the most beautiful and perfect day of their lives. When a loved one has died, the bereaved family and friends need you to show up and sit with them in their sorrow, and maybe offer some words of hope and consolation. Intimidating, to be sure, but there isn't a professional photographer circling the chancel as a memorial service unfolds.

Weddings elevate my natural tendency toward perfectionism to a new neurotic high. I want to do things properly. In my better moments, I remember that I am called to bear witness to the presence of God in all circumstances: joyous, mournful, quotidian. I was, and am, and surely forevermore will be humbled and honored to be invited into these moments. They are the heart of what it means to be human: life and love, death and loss.

Aiming to bear witness to God's presence in the safety of the sanctuary, cloaked in a robe and stole, and equipped with a liturgy for the occasion was one thing. Figuring out how to contribute anything holy or helpful to engaged couples during their required premarital counseling sessions was another animal altogether. I was woefully underprepared for my role. We had barely touched on the theory and practice of premarital counseling when I was a seminary student. If I had read all the assigned readings on the topic—and that's a big if, given my graduate school workload—I hadn't retained any of their wisdom. I'd meant to seek additional training; there are well-regarded premarital counseling models that help focus the sessions through questionnaires and conversation prompts. I have, in recent years, learned to lean on one of the better programs. But with all the stress and strain of my first years of ministry, I hadn't gotten around to it quite yet.

Accordingly, I prepared for Mitch and Josie's first premarital counseling session by grasping for the assistance that was readily available: I prayed for spiritual guidance, muttered "Amen," and Googled "premarital counseling." A limited and generic checklist of recommended topics to cover (sex, household chores, family of origin, etc.) became my map for our conversations. Not that I had yet figured out how to navigate these matters of significance in my own marriage. In addition to being a relatively new minister, I was also a relatively new married person. I had suffered from imposter syndrome all along, fretting that I would be exposed as a fraud in seminary, or perhaps during my ordination examination, or worst of all by the people who had called me (prayerfully, unanimously, joyfully) to be their pastor. I lacked wisdom and confidence; the best-case scenario was, in my mind, to get through my first few weddings without making a total fool of myself.

When the young and beautiful newly engaged couple showed up in my study hand in hand, expecting me to have something of value to offer, my sense of inadequacy skyrocketed. I could hardly contain my nerves as I asked them to tell me how they met; however was I to summon the courage to facilitate conversations about finances, inlaws, and—God forbid—*sex*? (Pardon me while I clutch my pearls.) Despite my apprehension, I enjoyed the time with Mitch and Josie. I did my best in our handful of premarital counseling sessions, and while the counsel I offered to them was certainly not excellent and probably not even passable, by the time July rolled around I felt connected to the couple and invested in their relationship. I spent hours crafting my homily for their wedding, and printed a copy on pretty paper as a low-budget wedding gift. I spent more hours rehearsing the logistics of the ceremony—so similar yet so different from the worship services I led for the congregation each Sunday. Charise, our newly hired church secretary, agreed to take on wedding coordinator responsibilities as well. Our nascent friendship was sealed as we bonded over the project of running a wedding rehearsal together. (Not long ago, when I told Charise I was writing a book about marriage, she responded, "For me, personally, marriage is always handing me something I wasn't prepared for. It's much more difficult than *%&# Nicholas Sparks makes it out to be." We hired well.)

The day of the wedding was one of the handful of days it would have been awfully nice to have air conditioning in the sanctuary; ordinarily, our proximity to the beach meant that the ocean winds ushered the heat eastward, toward the Los Angeles basin. But that afternoon it was so sweltering that I broke a sweat the instant I layered my preaching garments over my paper-thin sundress. Charise and I flitted around the sanctuary opening the windows and doors, a move we later regretted as we unsuccessfully attempted to clean up the smattering of candle wax the hot and unrefreshing breeze deposited on the new carpet. We manufactured multiple excuses to visit Josie in the bride's room, where an air conditioning unit had been cranked to such a degree that it approximated a walk-in refrigerator; the bridesmaids shivered in their chiffon gowns. We left Mitch and the groomsmen to suffer alone in the airless church library, which reeked of musty books when the temperature rose.

At the appointed time, the organist pulled out the stops for the prelude—my cue to lead the men to their places on the chancel for the pageantry to proceed. One by one, the bridesmaids emerged through the doors into the sanctuary. Josie, decked out to the nines in her designer gown, upswept red tresses, and flawless makeup, looked like she belonged on the cover of *Brides* magazine. It was a beautiful wedding, if I do say so myself. In retrospect, I should have trimmed a few paragraphs from the homily, as eloquence only goes so far when you are very, very hot. But as the bride and groom knelt

at the squeaky-clean wedding kneeler to receive their blessing and to be prayed for by their pastor and all their friends
and family, I marveled that I was finally starting to figure the
whole thing out. I was marrying people! People who would
live happily ever after, as husband and wife!

They divorced. Almost immediately.

I'm sad when any marriage ends, but selfishly I lamented
that one of the first couples I married had divorced. I knew,
intellectually, that my role in their relationship was incredibly
limited; they had moved to Seattle just weeks after their wedding, so I didn't have an ongoing pastoral relationship with
them. But I still wondered if I could have done anything differently to better prepare them for married life. That stupid
checklist of conversations starters I printed off the Internet
was clearly insufficient for the task, the gravity of which was
now ever more real to me. Perhaps if I'd been a premarital
counselor with training and experience, I might have even
discerned that they weren't well-suited to marry one another
after all. I suspect one way to prevent divorce is to forestall
poorly matched couples from marrying in the first place.
That being said, I am entirely unconvinced that the practice
of refusing to officiate a wedding for apparently incompat-
ible couples is effective for anything other than preserving
the pastor's conscience. (You know what they'll do once they
storm out of your office, right? Knock on the door of the
church down the street, or just scrap the idea of a church
wedding and make a date with a justice of the peace.)

I've kept in touch with Josie through the years. It's a funny
friendship; I was her pastor for a very short time, during
which she made one of the bigger mistakes of her life. This

connects us in a powerful way. I feel guilty for having done a better job of preparing the kneeler for the wedding than the bride and groom for the marriage; she feels guilty for having broken the sacred covenant I blessed. She doesn't fault me for not realizing her marriage would be a train wreck, and in turn, I don't fault her for leaving her train wreck of a marriage. According to Josie, Mitch wasn't the husband she thought she was getting; there is always a danger that one doesn't *really* know one's potential spouse, of course, but the risk of such a bait and switch is probably higher with quick courtships like Josie's (and, for that matter, mine). Mitch didn't approach marriage as a partnership of mutuality and compromise. He was rude and entitled, possessive and domineering. I suspect he thought he found in Josie the perfect trophy wife; the same beauty that intimidated me must have appealed to him.

In a sense, Mitch suffered a bait and switch too, because Josie very quickly realized that she didn't want to live her life as a subservient wife, forsaking her own dreams and desires to serve an unloving husband. But it was the thought of having children with Mitch that ultimately made her leave. Maybe she could have lived with a lousy husband, but she didn't want her children to have a lousy father.

Josie lays part of the blame on herself. Mitch was, after all, her second husband; her first marriage was equally brief and unhappy. "I ended up having relationships with the wrong people because I didn't really know who I was and had little sense of self-worth," she told me. "I made myself into someone else so that I could please these other people and make them want to be with me."

I've only heard one side of the story; I haven't spoken to Mitch since I shook his hand goodnight at their wedding reception. His version of their unraveling would no doubt diverge from Josie's. But I trust Josie, and I honor her account of their disastrous union. When she recounts that time in her life, she exhibits a sadness that reminds me of the psalmist's "broken and contrite heart."

For all my moralizing about the sacredness of matrimony and the tragedy of divorce, I don't have the heart to condemn someone for leaving an unredeemable marriage. If Josie and Mitch had turned up in my office again six months into marriage telling tales of hostility and contention, I would have strongly encouraged them to see a well-regarded marriage and family therapist and prayed that they would do everything they could to salvage their relationship. But if they tried (and tried, and tried, and tried) and failed, what good would it have done to pressure them to stick it out or to stand in judgment as they pursued separation? Sentencing someone to a lifetime of misery seems a remarkably cruel way to preserve the sanctity of marriage, even if they did promise to be parted only by death.

The writer Ann Patchett left her first husband just a year after they wed, despite the stalwart stance her Roman Catholic faith traditionally takes on divorce. She writes of her experience with ambivalence and regret but also with gratitude.

> Divorce is in the machine now, like love and birth and death. Its possibility informs us, even when it goes untouched. And if we fail at marriage, we are lucky we don't have to fail with the force of our whole life. I would like there to be an eighth sacrament: the sacrament of

divorce. Like communion, it is a slim white wafer on the tongue. Like confession, it is forgiveness. Forgiveness is important not so much because of what we've done wrong, but for what we feel we need to be forgiven for. Family, friends, God, whoever loves us, forgives us, takes us in again. They are thrilled by our life, our possibilities, our second chances. They weep with gladness that we did not have to die.[1]

I hold this paradox in tension: I lament Josie's divorce—and would have lamented it exponentially more had children been involved—but I am indeed thrilled by her life, her life without Mitch. I lament her divorce but am thrilled that through therapy and prayer, she learned to see herself as a child of God, forgiven and beloved. I lament her divorce but am thrilled she got a third chance: she is a wife again, only this time she is in a marriage marked by tenderness, affection, and abiding love. I lament her divorce but am thrilled that she is a mother. Yes, I weep with sorrow in the face of divorce. But I also weep with gladness that Josie did not have to die to extract herself from marriage. Marriage is holy, but maybe it's something like the Sabbath—made for humankind, not the other way around.

There is, in the liturgy book of the United Church of Christ, something like the "sacrament of divorce" Patchett longed to receive. It isn't called a sacrament; like many Protestants, only baptism and communion are considered official sacraments in the UCC. It is called an "Order for the Recognition of the End of a Marriage." I confess my kneejerk reaction is to roll my eyes at my unfailingly liberal adopted denomination.

But the ritual is actually a magnanimous and meaningful one. The introduction to the liturgy soberly explains,

> The service is penitential in nature and cannot be construed to be an encouragement of divorce or a depreciation of marriage. It does not celebrate the failure of a relationship, but acknowledges that a divorce has occurred and that two human beings are seeking in earnest to reorder their lives in a wholesome, redemptive way. The service is a reminder that nothing can separate people from the love of God in Jesus Christ.[2]

I haven't used the liturgy yet, but I would. It speaks the language of lamentation and confession, mercy and hope. It is deeply religious and utterly humane. It takes marriage seriously enough to acknowledge the gravity of a marriage's end, and to acknowledge it in community—even, perhaps, in the sacred space of a sanctuary. I first read the liturgy as I sat on my living room sofa, my legs entangled with Benjamin's. Even if I never don my robe and stole to preside over the dissolution of a marriage covenant, I suspect having these words echoing through my subconscious will make me a wiser pastor.

I read the liturgy a second time, this time intending to pray the prayers—for all the people who suspect their lives were saved by divorce, for all the people who imagine they could only ever receive judgment, not compassion, from a member of the clergy, for all the people who meant forever but didn't make it. For Josie. For Mitch.

God of all mercy,
we know that you love us even when we are not sure
that we love ourselves.
Embrace us when frustration and failure
leave us hollow and empty.
Forgive our sins,
and grant us forgiving hearts toward others.
In the confessions of our lips,
show us now the promise of a new day,
the springtime of the forgiven;
through Jesus Christ,
who is able to make all things new.
Amen.[3]

11

FLUNKING EPHESIANS 4:26

We were on our way home from a dinner date at a French restaurant, during which I stole bites of Benjamin's steak to supplement my vegetable tagine. There was no special occasion to celebrate, save that one of our favorite babysitters was leaving for college (the nerve!) and we wanted to give the girls one last night of convincing her to let them stay up past their bedtime to play board games. I was prattling on, as I am inclined to do, about some article I'd read that morning in the Sunday *New York Times* that filled me with dread for the state of the world, when I detected Benjamin's subtle shift from half listening to not listening to me at all. He had noticed jostling in the SUV stopped at the red light ahead of us. Violent jostling. The whole vehicle shook, apparently as some sort of violence exploded between the passenger and driver.

Benjamin was on high alert. As a case manager working in social service agencies, he has encountered enough domestic violence situations to fill him with dread for the state of the world; he doesn't need the newspaper for that. He pointed out the car and filled me in on what he had witnessed. As we approached the next red light, he planned to pull alongside it to ascertain if we should call the police. He hit the brakes as a man shot out of the passenger door, slammed it behind him, and charged in front of our Honda to the sidewalk. It was an insufferably hot August evening. The man, red-faced and seething with anger, stormed down the sidewalk. Through the tinted windows, we watched the woman behind the wheel wiping tears from her face. The light turned green, and she took off down the street erratically, cutting across lanes at the next intersection to make a last-minute right turn. We wondered if she was turning around to go back to him. We wondered if it was the first time violence flared in the space above the emergency brake. We wondered if it would be the last time.

It happened so quickly we didn't catch her license plate number, and we didn't know what we would tell the police if we did call. We couldn't even tell aggressor from victim. He could have hit her. She could have hit him. I didn't prattle anymore. Even I can be stunned into silence.

In her poem "Domestic Violence," Eavan Boland recalls overhearing a couple quarreling in the early days of her own marriage. She notes, "nothing is ever entirely / right in the lives of those who love each other."[1] This is the sort of line that keeps me reading poetry. I don't want it to be true and yet I know it is. It's not that *nothing* is ever right in the lives of those who love each other. It's just that nothing is ever *entirely* right. I sense in Boland's verse gratitude that she and her husband were not the quarreling couple, but it's not a self-congratulatory gratitude. It's a gratitude complicated by the reality that her marriage had concealed its own ugliness. That other couple screamed their acrimony for the neighbors to hear, but a whisper can deliver viciousness too. Every couple has to figure out how to cope with conflict, miscommunication, fleeting fury. You fight badly, or you fight well, or you fight the unwinnable battle of letting your fights fester unfought. But you fight.

When I think of our first few years of marriage, I think of driving to Santa Anita Park racetrack to spend a Saturday afternoon placing two-dollar bets on the thoroughbreds with the best names. I think of walking past palm trees and mansions to Video Paradiso in downtown Claremont, where we rented foreign films so frequently the workers knew our names. I think of showering together nearly every morning, to conserve water and to scrub one another's backs and to simply enjoy some good clean marital nudity before parting ways for the day.

And I think of the endless, awful, repetitive blowups that erupted between us over and over again. We were the ones upon whom the neighbors eavesdropped and quietly thanked their lucky stars that they were not.

We did not come to blows, save for the handful of times I smacked my own flesh in stupid, frantic rage. Neither of us was victim or perpetrator of physical violence against the other. This is not a given. Domestic violence is alarmingly common. I was warned in seminary that if I mentioned

spousal abuse in a sermon, I should be prepared to offer pastoral care and practical referrals to the women and men who
would be emboldened to speak up and seek help. And domestic violence is not infrequently deadly; women are far more
likely to be killed by a husband or boyfriend than a stranger.
As a pastor—and really, just as a human being—I try to be
educated about red flags. For instance, a woman who has
been strangled by a partner is seven times more likely to be
killed by him, yet strangling is frequently treated no more
seriously than a slap.[2] Many states are adopting relevant
legislation; a county solicitor in Georgia who was active in
the state's movement for expanded domestic violence laws
explained that when an abuser chokes his victim, he's sending
a clear message: "I have the ability to kill you."[3]

I do not mean to minimize the enormity of physical abuse.
I reiterate: neither Benjamin nor I was a victim or perpetrator of such terror. But I cannot say that our fights were not
without violence. They were too frightening, too destructive,
too fundamentally disordered to be correctly characterized
as *nonviolent*. We loved one another, but nothing was ever
entirely right, and was often closer to entirely wrong.

With several years of relative peace since we gradually
ceased regular hostilities, I can see patterns that were hidden
when I wept in the midst of it. Often, an argument arose
when something was hard. We couldn't get our campfire
started in Big Sur. We couldn't muster enough guidebook
French to order a brie and pear sandwich at the café near the
Champs-Élysées. We couldn't figure out how to fit the Ikea
bed frame through the door of the master bedroom on moving day. (Insert seven to ten more arguments directly related

to buying and/or building Ikea furniture.) We missed our exit on the interstate. We had a baby.

Whatever the precipitating challenge, it went down the same way: Benjamin lashed out at me in frustration. I lost my everloving mind in turn, indignation flooding my system. My responses confirmed Benjamin's subconscious conviction that it wasn't safe to be wrong, to be incapable, to make a mistake, to not know. Benjamin invariably wanted to walk away from the clash, which set off my own irrational fear of disconnection and abandonment. I mercilessly demanded he stay when he was desperate to leave, often blocking his path to the door. I pressed for elusive resolutions. I unapologetically asked for forgiveness with the express purpose of forcing a reciprocal apology. The apostle Paul encourages those who have new life in Christ to "be angry but do not sin; do not let the sun go down on your anger." We were flunking Ephesians 4:26. We were angry and we sinned in our anger. The sun went down and the constellations lit up the night skies and we remained in the thrall of our mutual fury. The fights would finally end when we were too spent to keep fighting. We would be so tired we could hardly remember what we were fighting about.

But we weren't, after all, fighting about the wet firewood, the French we couldn't pronounce, the bed that didn't fit, the missed exit, the inscrutability of a colicky newborn. We were fighting out of insecurity, laziness, immaturity, fear. Benjamin's untreated depression and my own tendency toward anxiety made matters far worse. But more than any other single factor, I reckon we were fighting out of habit. We had good reason to expect conversations to go south quickly;

they usually did. We assumed the worst of one another and responded to the most innocuous comments accordingly. We just could not be on the same team to save our lives, let alone our marriage.

I remember a particularly brutal exchange on our marriage counselor's couch. We were fighting about our fighting, which, in retrospect, was probably sowing the seeds of healing and reconciliation. I finally confessed what I really wanted: for Benjamin to be as kind and caring toward me as my best friend was. The therapist reminded me that my best friend had the benefit of not having to live with me. There were boundaries and distances in our platonic relationship that made it entirely distinct from the relentless proximity and intimacy of marriage. This is such an obvious nugget of common sense I'm embarrassed to admit that I received it as pure revelation. Marriage was unlike any other relationship I'd known. Being a wife required something entirely new from me; it was not the same as being a daughter, a sister, a girlfriend. It was not even the same as being a friend. It was more than all of this. Yet my confession was my conviction. I wanted Benjamin to treat me like a friend, but my contemptuous and antagonistic ways with him were anything but friendly. They were antithetical to friendship, and they were antithetical to love.

Not long ago I read an essay on the *Huffington Post*. As a general rule I avoid *HuffPo* at all costs, as it tends to be noisy, with some of the most uncharitable comment sections on the Internet (and that's really saying something). But the title was irresistible: "How I Saved My Marriage." The author, novelist Richard Paul Evans, describes a marriage that rivaled the cantankerousness of my own. He and his wife were continually at sixes and sevens, locked into a domestic war that could never be won. He writes,

> Finally, hoarse and broken, I sat down in the shower and began to cry. In the depths of my despair powerful inspiration came to me. You can't change her, Rick. You can only change yourself. At that moment I began to pray. If I can't change her, God, then change me. I prayed late into the night. I prayed the next day on the flight home. I prayed as I walked in the door to a cold wife who barely even acknowledged me. That night, as we lay in our bed, inches from each other yet miles apart, the inspiration came. I knew what I had to do.[4]

What he did was ask his wife the next morning what he could do to help her have a better day. At first she didn't trust him, and why would she? On the second day she tried to test him, asking him to clean the garage before he went to work. He persisted. With time, the practices of care and attention and servanthood became mutual. They became a husband and wife who were for, not against, one another. I love the essay not only because it tells a redemption story and bears testimony to the transformative power of prayer. I love it because the question that Evans asked his wife—the question that was the seed of reconciliation—is so revealing. No one has more power to make your day better, or worse, than your spouse. Happy wife, happy life. (I'm not trying to be sexist; I'd equitably extend the aphorism but nothing rhymes with *husband*, a fact I confirmed in my trusty rhyming dictionary.)

The Evans essay squares with scientific research about conflict and communication in marriage. John Gottman first began studying marriage seriously in the 1970s, when sky-rocketing divorce rates caught the attention of sociologists. Gottman became so good at analyzing the communication between couples that he could predict, at the creepily accurate rate of *more than 91 percent*, whether couples would remain married after observing them interact for a mere five minutes. (I reckon I could guess how Gottman would have deemed our chances had he been a fly on our seminary apartment wall.) In his enormously popular book coauthored with Nan Silver, Gottman endeavors to educate couples to identify and correct toxic patterns. I don't favor the pop psychology or self-help genre, but *The Seven Principles for Making Marriage Work: A Practical Guide from the Country's Foremost Relationship Expert* is a book worth reading and rereading. I keep copies on my bookshelf at home and in my study at church. While it doesn't do justice to the fullness of Gottman's work, if I were to boil his teaching down to a singular edict, it this: be kind.

In an essay about Gottman's work for the *Atlantic* online, Emily Esfahani Smith writes, "There are two ways to think about kindness. You can think about it as a fixed trait: either you have it or you don't. Or you could think of kindness as a muscle. In some people, that muscle is naturally stronger than in others, but it can grow stronger in everyone with exercise."[5] This is the muscle Richard Paul Evans rediscovered after a night on his knees in prayer, and this is the muscle Benjamin and I continue to strengthen, little by little, day by day.

We still fight. But we fight far less frequently and far more gracefully. We are learning the art of restraint and the craft of forgiveness. And I suspect that all the hard work we have done in this relationship has effects well beyond our household. Despite the uniqueness of marriage, lessons learned within this singular covenant translate to other relationships. Marriage has required me to face the very same insecurities and weaknesses that dogged several other important relationships in my life. To be sure, I can still get defensive and petty and critical. (You may now picture my dear old dad nodding enthusiastically.) But I know myself in a way that only the mirror of marriage could have shown me.

Not long ago a friend shared a link to an article published in Focus on the Family's *Thriving Family* magazine. The article is short and sweet; in it, a mother asks her young daughter to read 1 Corinthians 13, swapping out the word *love* for the name of the cute boy she likes.[6] The girl realizes that the cute boy isn't, in fact, patient and kind. He is arrogant and rude, and all the other things Paul says love is not. The mother goes on to ask her daughter to consider her own name in the verses. And this, for me, is the key. It is easy enough to ask if Benjamin is irritable or resentful. But am I? Am I patient and kind? Do I keep a record of wrongs? If I flunk all those biblical tests of love in my own marriage—my own *marriage*!—then I flunk them outright.

If a Christian has a calling to live a life of love—a life modeled after the ways of Jesus and rooted in the great commandments to love God and neighbor—a married Christian is first and foremost charged to live this life within his or her own household. The correct answer to the question "Who is my neighbor?" is, of course, everyone. This is why reading the newspaper is, for me, an exercise in lamentation; this is why we contemplated calling the police when violence erupted in our midst. But a spouse is the neighbor of nearest proximity, the neighbor who demands the most of you, the neighbor with whom you share a heck of a lot more than a property line.

I wanted my husband to treat me like a cherished friend, but what I needed was to treat my husband like a beloved neighbor.

12

WITH MY BODY, I THEE WORSHIP

A few years ago, as an entrée to the somber season of Lent, I organized a public reading of the gospel of Mark—the whole book, all in one sitting. It was such a compelling encounter with sacred Scriptures that I intend to cook up a sequel. This time I'll find a married couple courageous enough to try a readers theater with Song of Songs—the book of the Bible that is almost entirely composed of a sensual exchange between lovers. I confess I shall delight to see my parishioners' cheeks redden as the woman reads, from one of those Bibles bound in red leather and gilded in gold, "With great delight I sat in his shadow, and his fruit was sweet to my taste" (Song of Songs 2:3). You do not need to be a biblical scholar to guess what sort of fruit she might have been sampling.

In the New Testament, sex is often appraised with suspicion. Paul writes in his first letter to the Corinthians, "Do not
deprive one another except perhaps by agreement for a set
time, to devote yourselves to prayer, and then come together
again, so that Satan may not tempt you because of your lack
of self-control. This I say by way of concession, not of command" (1 Corinthians 7:5-6). Paul seems to be saying, "Well,
if you *must*." In a perfect world, followers of Christ would
be celibate like Paul, like Jesus. Throughout much of the
Hebrew Bible, sex is intertwined with violence. One might
argue that more biblical ink is spilled on the countless ways
that sex can be exploited and misused than on affirming the
beauty of sexual union. Certainly, the early church fathers,
with all their Hellenistic influences, took it upon themselves
to construct a Christianity distrustful of flesh—a rather ironic
turn of events, considering that the core of the faith is a story
of God becoming flesh. You can easily piece together how
the church came to have a reputation for being uncomfortable with human sexuality. Perhaps even outright hostile to
it. Still, you can't very well valorize family without tolerating
a certain activity associated with reproduction.

Sex is how we all came to be, yet we have a tendency
to compulsively secret it under layers of myth and shame—
except, of course, when it might be useful for the marketing
of consumer goods. No one is selling anything in the remarkable sex-positive Song of Songs. No one is coercing. No one
is shaming. I completely adore that the intimacies between
the lovers in the Song of Songs are still capable of making
people blush thousands of years later. I suspect the power

of these love letters is in their frankness, their honesty, their utter shamelessness.

The story of these lovers is true, and the story of these lovers is good. I worry that there aren't enough true stories going around. I know there aren't enough good stories going around.

I'm biased, but I think our story—that is, the story of Benjamin's and my life together as lovers—is both true and good. The problem is that I don't particularly want to tell it. And you, dear reader, don't particularly want to hear it. Modesty is a virtue I don't have in spades, but when it comes to telling tales of the bedroom, I'm overwhelmed by the impulse to draw the shades, to speak in generalities, to tell you to just read Song of Songs with your own lover—and leave me and my lover out of it.

We spent the early married years trying to figure it all out. What felt good (physically, emotionally). What hurt (physically, emotionally). We stepped into minefields we knew about, and even more we didn't. We identified where our natural boundaries fell, and discerned whether it was worth it to transgress them for a fleeting thrill. We learned to live within the extraordinary intimacy of sharing our whole selves with another. The juxtapositions of marriage are intense: in any given day, you eat and worship and fight and—well. You know.

And then we had kids. This is a story that has been told, and told again. The body changes; parts of my body that used to be for *this* were now for *that*. There was pain that lasted longer than the tidy six weeks women are given to heal. Desire died an untimely death and, upon resurrection, was rudely interrupted by the wails or wafts of dirty diapers from the little ones who were the lovely by-product of sex.

My children are growing, and there will be no more (Lord willing, and the contraceptives don't fail). Benjamin and I have experienced a slow shifting from the childbearing years to a new chapter—a chapter in which the children are still young yet no longer prevail upon my body in nearly so needy a fashion. It turns out that desire as we once knew it did die, but that this is a good thing. There is a new iteration of desire, and it's better. It turns out that even the most extraordinary intimacies of our pre-kid days pale in comparison. Maybe I would miss my twentysomething body if I weren't so much more capable of being naked in my thirtysomething skin.

Not long ago I pulled together a panel of married people to share their stories and wisdom about marriage with a group of young moms in my congregation. Two of the couples had been married about thirty years; the third, a whopping fifty-four. I asked the veteran couples questions that I had solicited from the women in the moms' group.

One question made us all laugh: "What can a woman do to make her husband feel loved—excluding boom boom?" (We never explicitly defined the term *boom boom*, but I've been told by several folks present that day that the slang has been added to their personal lexicons.) A man on the panel immediately quipped, "Nothing!" One of the women, Pamela, admitted that, in her experience and from what she heard from many of her friends, it did seem like sex was especially important to men. Sometimes she just plain didn't feel like doing it, but she had decided early in her marriage that it was worth it to engage in physical intimacy anyway.

She pondered the notion that, at least sometimes, sex can be given as a gift.

Some might bristle at the thought of offering a sexual favor the same way one might wrap up a new pair of slippers. But a well-given gift gives delight to both giver and recipient. Pamela wants to make her beloved husband happy, and sex is a fairly surefire way to accomplish this particular goal. And, Pamela added, it's not like she "grits her teeth and braces herself" while they have sex; much of the time she ends up just as aroused as her more libidinous husband.

Her experience squares with the work of therapist and researcher Michele Weiner-Davis, author of the bestselling book *The Sex-Starved Marriage: Boosting Your Marriage Libido*. This is the sort of title one might prefer to purchase as an ebook. If your moderately embarrassing self-help books are in digital form, you can read them on the train undetected. For all the other passengers know, you could be digging into *The Brothers Karamazov*. Unfortunately, I was not in possession of an electronic reader on November 6, 2008, which is, according to my Amazon purchase history, the date I ordered the book. (Our first daughter was born in early 2008; there was a definite correlation, if not outright causation, between her birth and my furtive Amazon shopping expedition.)

I read the book in a day. Most helpful to me was Weiner-Davis's explanation of the distinction between *desire* and *arousal*, and the different ways the two can work in tandem. Some people desire sex, she explains, and then get aroused. Others have to experience arousal before desire sets in—which is to say, ten minutes into foreplay you find yourself wanting more of the very thing you pondered putting off.

Perhaps I should have pieced this together; I had quite a lot of field experience in the matter. But I could not connect the dots on my own.

Maybe it wasn't so unfortunate I bought the paperback edition after all. It's complicated to lend out an ebook, and my dog-eared copy of *The Sex-Starved Marriage* has, against all odds, been passed around quite a lot among my female parishioners. The first time a church member came into my office to discuss her increasingly celibate marriage, I hesitated for a moment before offering up my personal copy of the book. It seemed a little weird, no? But the book was a godsend to Benjamin and me, and I figured the awkwardness of lending my copy was worth the possibility it could be a godsend for her too.

A few months later, I checked in with my parishioner and asked if she was ready to return the book. She'd lent it to another church friend, who had passed it on to another. It's been making the rounds ever since.

On the panel, Kenneth, Pamela's aforementioned libidinous husband, added his perspective. He believed that men have a tendency to feel close to their wives *after* sex, and that women need intimacy to *precede* sex. Though many of the women in the room murmured in agreement, I wonder if such a theory holds true universally. I suspect that there are plenty of people who trespass against gender stereotypes, and Michele Weiner-Davis is careful to address the reality that female partners are frequently the ones complaining about not enough sex. Still, over the course of their nearly thirty years of marriage, Kenneth and Pamela had identified the patterns that, at the very least, pertained to their own relationship.

They had developed an understanding of their own needs and wants, as well as an understanding of one another's. This isn't the sort of awareness that happens during the course of a couple's honeymoon; it's the consequence of years of love and attention, trial and error. The women in the room—myself included—all seemed filled with relief and hope as we listened to this couple. We were witnessing a couple who approached "boom boom" with intelligence, compassion, and a clear intention to honor one another. They advised us to take sex seriously and joyfully. "Sex is what makes your relationship unique," Kenneth added as a closing remark.

A given: sexual relationships change over time. When boredom or conflict or changing bodies or a shift in desire cause a couple's boom boom to turn a bit humdrum, the onus is on the two of them to rediscover their passion for the one to whom they have pledged their troth. "Spicing up" your sex life is rarely as simple as *Cosmopolitan* magazine makes it; the spices that work are creativity and imagination, open-ness and vulnerability, honesty and perseverance. (The ubiq-uitous spice that does not work: pornography, which, like infidelity, ruinously fixes gaze, attention, and imagination elsewhere.) There is a beauty in the timeworn bond between lovers, a certain glory in a man finding the same woman sexy at thirty, forty, fifty—and vice versa. My marriage is made of fallow seasons and frisky nights, eras of eroticism and waves of tenderness. I am grateful for all of it, but especially for what remains the same: that it is only and ever he and I. Seeking to love one another well, with mind, and heart, and soul, and body.

As the captivating Masterpiece drama *Downton Abbey* turned the corner into its final season, Carson, the irreproachable butler with Victorian values and impeccable manners, proposes marriage to Mrs. Hughes, the sensible, warm, and principled head housekeeper. They are a perfect match; frankly, I can't imagine many other women tolerating Carson's idiosyncrasies. (Having compatible quirks, penchants, and proclivities goes a long way in marriage.) By her own admission, Mrs. Hughes and her betrothed are in "late middle age," and it is her aging body that fuels Mrs. Hughes's anxiety about the marriage. In one of the most awkward moments ever to air on television, Mrs. Hughes enlists her friend Mrs. Patmore, the cook, to find out if Carson intends for them to consummate the marriage, or if Carson and "Mrs. Carson" will merely be really friendly roommates.

The conversation between Carson and the cook is hilarious, because Mrs. Patmore cannot bring herself to bring up such indelicacies with her prim and proper boss. (Perhaps it would have been easier for her if she had the neologism *boom boom* in her apron pocket.) Ultimately, Carson pries the real matter out of her and sends the cook back to the kitchen with an unambiguous message for his fiancée: "Tell her, Mrs. Patmore, that in my eyes she is beautiful. She asks if I want a full marriage and the answer is yes, I do. I want a real marriage, a true marriage, with everything that that involves." This bit of romantic drama makes the old Anglican prayer book vows Carson and Mrs. Hughes exchange soon thereafter all the more poignant—"With my body, I thee worship," Carson pledges to his resplendent bride.

I love those old vows. They may harken back to an era in which sex was a forbidden subject, but they are far more incarnational—far more *carnal*—than the contemporary vow "to have and to hold." That old language acknowledges that there is a dimension of marriage—real marriage, true marriage—that is wondrously physical. It's about *bodies*. (Mrs. Patmore just blushed again.) And it's about worship. Sex, at its best, is not so dissimilar to worship. There is healing, connection, elation. A giving of self for the pleasure of the other. It is awkward and humbling, romantic and moving. It can become rote—but if you keep showing up through the dry spells, you leave yourself open to the possibility of renewal.

Perhaps the affinity between sex and worship is the best argument, for Christians anyway, for monogamy in marriage. We are monotheistic in our religion, monogamous in our relationships. No gods before God; no lovers on the side.

Communion, consummation.

I am my lover's, and my lover is mine.

13

THE SAME
CHOICE

I was sitting in a vegetarian café with my husband and another couple. We'd chatted all together on the way to the restaurant, but now, as we waited for our burritos and salads, I spoke with the woman and Benjamin was deeply absorbed in conversation with the man. I'd only met the woman the day before; she was the wife of a friend. She was the wife of *the* friend, the male friend who had, some months before, evoked in me a fierce and unexpected infatuation. (Oh, did I not mention that he is also married?)

Lest the surreal nature of this scenario pass you by, I repeat: That guy. His wife. My husband. And me. Eating hummus together as if it were the most natural thing in the world. And on one level, it was. I had been drawn to this man because he fascinated and delighted me. He is the kind of person I want to be around. So it should have been no surprise that I would find his wife equally fascinating and delightful, and that my husband would be charmed by the pair of them. Still, I was a bit twitterpated by the whole situation. A wave of guilt had set me stuttering as I shook hands with his wife at our first meeting. I felt embarrassed, ashamed. But I had not betrayed this lovely woman any more than I had betrayed my husband. I had honored my marriage vows and hers. Theirs. I set my discomfort aside and focused on getting to know her as a real, three-dimensional person and not merely an abstraction.

When I met this man, I struggled against wanting what I didn't want to want. But I also wanted to be friends with him, and this earnest inclination had not been totally corrupted by my initial conflation of connection with attraction. I didn't want to turn around and run the other way. I wanted to practice impeccable fidelity to my husband, and I wanted to do this without opting out of what seemed to be a potentially meaningful friendship.

Shortly after we met, I had casually mentioned to my new friend that I wished we could share a meal with our respective spouses someday. At the time I assumed this was a pipe dream that would never actually happen, given that we lived several hundred miles apart. It just seemed, in a perfect world, that becoming "couple friends" was the perfect solution. It would take our connection out of a precarious place of privacy and make our spouses witnesses to—even participants in—our friendship. And now, thanks to a literary festival that had drawn us to the same city, the improbable meal was being brought to our table by a hip dreadlocked waitress even as I threw my head back and laughed, with the man and his wife, at a joke Benjamin cracked at my expense.

While we were all in the same place at the same time, I paid close attention to my heart. It still leaped a bit too quickly when I caught sight of him. But the chemistry that had so startled me during our previous encounter had dissipated. I no longer felt an illicit, mysterious energy drawing an unwanted ring around us. Rather, I sensed a comfortable space between us—call it room for the Holy Spirit, if you will—and that on either side of that space we were each encircled by our marriages.

A thoughtful Christian friend worried about me telling this part of our story. "Are you giving others who can't trust themselves permission?" she asked me. "I could think of women I know who'd read this and might say, *see*? And they shouldn't see." I certainly hope she's wrong. If she's right, the consequences could be dire for those who "shouldn't see"—and damning for me. "If any of you put a stumbling block before one of these little ones who believe in me, it would be better for you if a great millstone were fastened around your neck and you were drowned in the depth of the sea," Jesus warns (Matthew 18:6). It horrifies me to think of my story becoming a stumbling block catapulting people toward infidelity, but it saddens me to think of withholding such an intricately beautiful chapter in my marriage. I offer this story, therefore, with fear and trembling, praying that it may not become fuel for sin, but that it may only and ever give glory to God.

On July 13, 2002, I promised to be faithful to my husband, *forsaking all others*. I'd never fully considered the implications of that phrase, tucked into the wedding liturgy of the Book of Common Prayer. *Forsaking* is a fierce, uncompromising word. To be forsaken is to be abandoned, deserted. When Jesus was on the cross, moments before he died, he cried out, "My God, my God, why have you forsaken me?" (Matthew 27:46b). It seems quietly radical to ask brides and grooms, as they stand together before God and grandmother, to swear to forsake all others. It is an altogether different thing than to ask them to "be careful about boundaries" or other such polite language. Those vows to forsake all others are not messing around—and neither should one who has constructed his or her life within the sacred covenant they fashion. The subtext of that pledge is this: Your marriage comes first. Don't plunge your hand into the adder's den. Flee from anything—or anyone—that might cause cracks in the foundation of your marriage. To be faithful to the one who is your husband is to forsake the one who is not.

"So, Katherine," you might ask, "should you *really* still be friends with this guy?" And this is a fair question.

There is a part of me that wonders if the answer should be a firm negative. I think of an acquaintance of mine who was once a vocal proponent of cross-gender friendships. He told idyllic tales of how he and his female best friend enjoyed the trust and blessings of their respective spouses. He believed that the church unwisely conspired to quell friendships between men and women, and that a puritanical culture robbed people of deep and abiding platonic joy. He scoffed at those who clucked their tongues and warned of temptation. It wasn't inevitable, of course. Plenty of friendships are just that, and do not become something else. But in this

case temptation did rear its ugly head, and his entirely platonic intimacy was abruptly restyled into a full-blown affair.
Divorces were swiftly sought. As soon as they were legally
cleared to do so, the formerly platonic friends remarried. He
doesn't talk about cross-gender friendship so much anymore.

Wesley Hill, the eminently likeable author of *Spiritual
Friendship: Finding Love in the Church as a Celibate Gay
Christian*, contributes another layer of nuance. Being neither
celibate nor gay, nor of the conviction that gay and lesbian
Christians should refrain from establishing loving and intimate same-sex relationships, I did not immediately consider
myself part of his primary readership. But there is much in
the slender volume that speaks to me. Hill's perennial quandary is this: As a Christian committed to celibacy, cultivating deep friendships in lieu of romantic relationships is an
appealing antidote to loneliness. Hill knows from painful
personal experience that he is susceptible to desiring more
than mere friendship from his close confidants. Yet surely the
answer is not to shun friendship as a gateway drug to erotic
entanglement. It is one thing to practice celibacy, yet another
to live a life of isolation.

Still, certain friendships, for Hill, will involve risk and
require boundaries. "My question, at root, is how I can stew-
ard and sanctify my homosexual orientation in such a way that
it can be a doorway to blessing and grace," he writes. "For my
part, living with this question has meant cultivating greater
self-awareness. I've had to learn to face, rather than run away
from, the attractions I've developed for certain male friends
over the years. I have not only had to learn to admit these feelings to myself, to see them for what they are and acknowledge

their complexity, but I have also had to find appropriate confessors and wise pastoral guides who can listen to me and tease out the significance of what I'm feeling."[1]

I can't claim that there is a tidy parallel between the experiences of a celibate gay man and those of a married straight woman. There is, however, a resonance. The safest choice for Hill and for me would be to extract ourselves from any relationship that has tempted us to cede our respective vows of chastity (celibacy in singleness; fidelity in marriage). Frankly, in many cases I suspect the safest choice is also the wisest choice. But sometimes the safest choice is not the most faithful choice; as Hill's priest says, "When have Christians ever believed in playing it safe?"[2] I had to laugh at this; even if it is at odds with my Christian faith, I nearly always prefer playing it safe.

If I believed the friendship was inherently toxic—if I fretted that it was a hazard capable of undoing the life I love—I would forsake it in a second. But I do not. Nor does Benjamin. A shift of seismic proportions happened the night I admitted the temptation to my husband. It isn't that every ounce of malapropos emotion scattered immediately; if I swore that it did, I would make a liar of myself, and in these complicated and murky waters, absolute candor is critical. It's that I made my choice. It was the same choice I made all those years ago, the same choice I made last week, and this morning, and expect to make all the days of my life: I choose fidelity. I choose to love my husband first and most. I choose to be true. Because Benjamin trusts me, I choose to be worthy of that trust. But I don't rely on my good intentions alone. I seek wise counsel from my closest girlfriends, my pastor, my spiritual director. I pray. Before the big reunion, I whispered "God, go before me," and I was comforted by a deep sense of God's presence and guidance.

The consequence of this hard and holy work is freedom. In his letter to the Romans, Paul expounds on the nature of Christian freedom. "But thanks be to God that you, having once been slaves of sin, have become obedient from the heart to the form of teaching to which you were entrusted, and that you, having been set free from sin, have become slaves of righteousness" (Romans 6:17-18). I have felt, with bewildered gratitude, the peculiar joy of exchanging death for life—sin for righteousness. I find that my affection and regard for my friend, and for his dear wife, is far more lasting than the infatuation. By taking the risk of remaining friends, I—we—reap the benefit of having two fine people in our lives, however infrequently we may convene or communicate. In Christ, the crush is forsaken, the friendship redeemed. In Christ, my faith is renewed, my marriage strengthened.

After we warmly parted ways with our new friends, Benjamin was characteristically quiet in the car. Even though I've known him for all these years, I still can't consistently discern one sort of silence from another; he has several in rotation. I tentatively tried to assess his mood. Was he weirded out? Jealous? Riding another wave of hurt? It didn't seem so. And so I dared ask him what I really wanted to know: *Do you understand why, now that you've met him?*

Yes, he said. He understood.

We held hands the rest of the way home.

14

MEMENTO MORI

I was in Texas when I realized my husband was dying. I wouldn't be able to get home to him for days. I would have to ring him up to inform him over the phone, which seemed a deeply inappropriate means of communicating such a prognosis. Surely a phone call was not commensurate with the gravity of the situation. I presume that when doctors break the news to terminal patients, they are delicate about it. They invite the moribund men and women to change out of their immodest hospital gowns so that they might learn of their demise while clothed in the dignity of their own trousers. But then, I'm not a doctor. I don't know how to tell someone he is dying.

My fears of Benjamin's imminent death were extreme and unhealthy but not entirely irrational. We had learned the prior year that he could have inherited a genetic disorder that vastly increases one's likelihood of developing a number of different types of cancers. The news was passed along with an encouragement to take a simple DNA test to determine if he had the same cancer risk as the average person, or if he had a lifetime of invasive scans and scopes and blood draws ahead of him. Heads, Lynch syndrome. Tails, we could breathe a lot easier. A precisely fifty-fifty chance of potential loss or luck.

Benjamin hadn't yet made it to the lab to have his cheek swabbed when I boarded a plane and flew to Austin, Texas, for the better part of the week. The first day of the story-telling conference started with a bang: we were sorted into small groups and charged with the small project of swapping life stories. Before we began, we sat quietly for a half hour to think through what we wanted to say, to remember our lives before we gave voice to them. At each turning point, the instructor directed, consider what it was you were yearning for.

As I thought through the tangles of my early years, recalling the fraught and tiresome phases of my youth, I was positively overcome when I came to the part in my story in which Benjamin became a primary character. We had recently celebrated our tenth anniversary. We have had no lack of struggles in our years together, but I felt a renewed sense of gratitude that he is the person with whom I have promised to spend my life. I felt deeply glad for the gift of our marriage. When I told my story to the four people in my small group, I said as much. I planned to tell Benjamin when I spoke to him later—not that I don't frequently tell him I love him. I just planned to tell him I *really* love him.

And then the next storyteller recalled the horrors of her nearly fatal brush with one of the cancers with which Lynch syndrome is most closely identified. As she spoke, I began to panic. When all you have is a hammer, everything looks like a nail, and when you're having a sudden-onset fit of acute hypochondria, everything looks like a symptom. Even the innocuous nap Benjamin had taken on Sunday afternoon became evidence of oncological fatigue.

I slipped my phone in my pocket and excused myself. Benjamin picked up on the first ring; my cheeks were already streaked with tears. The panic clutched my throat, turning my voice into an unintelligible squeal. Poor Benjamin presumed something awful had happened, but I caught my breath and conjugated: something awful *will* happen. In fact, it was already happening, even as we spoke: malignancies multiplying, a cellular mutiny in his large intestines. It had probably already metastasized to his liver—or, heaven forbid, his brain. He could have six months. He could have six *weeks*.

There was indeed a steep chance that Benjamin had the syndrome and, if so, a corollary possibility that the syndrome had already begun sabotaging the division and multiplication of his cells. But once it dawned on me that it was feasible that Benjamin had cancer—well, you would have been hard-pressed to convince me that he was not riddled with prodromes or that the prognosis was anything but dire. My husband was both shaken and a bit annoyed by my spontaneous and hysterical diagnosis. He agreed that the thing to do would be to get tested as soon as possible, to both assuage my fear and rule out the possibility that I was right.

I was wrong, thank God. Benjamin wasn't dying, except in the sense that he wasn't busy being born and was therefore, according to Bob Dylan, busy dying. I wouldn't have confirmation of my misdiagnosis for almost a full month. Almost a full month I spent convinced I would soon be a widow, the mother of fatherless daughters. Almost a full month wracked with uncontrollable anxiety, premature grief, and increasingly sophisticated Internet searches for more information about Lynch syndrome and the cancers correlated with it. Forget Wikipedia; I was poking around on websites written by, and clearly for, medical professionals. When the jargon got too thick, I tortured myself by compulsively returning to a legacy fundraising site, where I searched for clues in the story of the thirtysomething husband and father of two who died, swiftly and miserably, from the very cancer I was certain was growing within my thirtysomething husband and father of two. I never found what I was looking for, because what I was looking for was confirmation that Benjamin would not die. Preferably ever. But I would have settled for the assurance that he would not die of cancer within the year. Perhaps this promise would be hidden in the footnotes of an obscure British medical journal. It couldn't hurt to look.

There is nothing more uncertain than death, except, of course, that it will most certainly happen. But we don't know when (mercifully) and we don't know how (again, mercifully). It's enough to make me feel a bit dumb. Since I don't let my children say that word, let me rephrase: it's enough to make me feel *humbled*.

Most people do a lot to avoid thinking about death. We secret it away in hospitals, we scroll through Facebook, we smear ourselves with wrinkle creams. But death cannot be avoided. Death cannot be outsmarted. Even those of us who have been captivated by the astonishing story of a loving God who vanquishes death will, sooner or later, breathe our last.

As a pastor, I have commended many a soul to the everlasting care of God, and I have spent hours with their loved ones who remain. Not long ago, I sat with a grieving widow. Her husband was long gone, having died several years before. By this point she was supposed to be playing bridge, or strapping on her fanny pack to travel to Tuscany, or flirting with the widower in the apartment next door. She would have none of it. She wept openly, practically keening beneath the weight of her loss. "Oh," she moaned. "Oh, I loved him so much." Blessed are those who mourn, said Jesus, but it rarely ever seems that way.

There is an ancient Latin phrase: *memento mori*. It means "remember you will die." The reminder has been woven into Christian music, liturgy, and art. The most famous artifacts of the memento mori tradition are paintings and sculptures of human skulls. They are morbid, but that's the point. They exist to shake you out of your bubble of naïveté and remind you of your inevitable demise. These frank reminders of death are invaluable. Everybody dies, and therefore everybody has some critical choices to make about how to live. The theory is that having the courage to contemplate death frees us to fully embrace the gift of life. So long as I'm not asked to contemplate dying before my children are all grown up, I might conjure the courage to be philosophical about my own passing. My favorite Mary Oliver poem includes a stirring memento mori: "Doesn't everything die at last, and too soon?"[1] I get a thrill. Surely I will do wondrous things with my "one wild and precious life."

But. When forced to contemplate my not-quite-middle-aged husband's death, I didn't do so with any equanimity, or philosophy, or poetry. I did so with fear and anxiety, dread and despair. I did pray, or at least I think I prayed. Is it prayer, after all, to scream *please* in one's car until one's throat is hoarse and one's capacity to cry is spent? It wasn't the first time I had been swept up in debilitating anxiety about death. It had taken a lot of work to cope with the reality that my daughters are not immune to it. I couldn't fathom how a mother could get out of bed in the morning knowing that her children were vulnerable to death, as well as any number of unthinkable dangers. All the grooves in my brain where the anxiety loops play were at the ready for this new broken record.

The fact of Benjamin's mortality had darted past me before, when we were newlyweds. One morning I woke early, or what constituted early in the lazier mornings of my graduate school rhythms. I was shrouded in a tangle of sheets and limbs. In the gray light and emerging wakefulness, I considered, sadly but with remarkable equanimity, that one day Benjamin's arms would be cold and stiff and I wouldn't feel the warmth of his breath on my neck and he would be dead. Or maybe I would die first. Who could know? We watched a lot of *Six Feet Under* in those days. A character dies at the beginning of every episode. You get used to it.

How different it was to consider his death again, and while irrationally convinced of its imminence. A decade and offspring made it an unbearable prospect. (To be sure, my anxiety issue that occasionally spikes above the point at which it is responsible to leave it untreated contributed as well.) I fumed that I hadn't even needed this particular memento mori to remember the precious and singular bond of our love; I'd already been dwelling on my endearment for him and for our life together.

When I consider eschatology in the Bible, it's not the fiery lakes of the book of Revelation that unnerve me most. I'm well versed enough in apocalyptic literature to know that these images aren't meant to be interpreted literally. What truly rattles me is Jesus' response to the Sadducees' query about marriage in the resurrection, a conversation that takes place in all three synoptic gospels. The Sadducees propose a moderately ridiculous scenario: the same woman outliving seven ill-fated husbands. "In the resurrection," they ponder, "whose wife will she be?"

The question is meant to stump Jesus. His answer is startling: he essentially tells them they're asking the wrong question. "For when they rise from the dead," Jesus says in Mark's version, "they neither marry nor are given in marriage, but are like angels in heaven" (Mark 12:25).

Is this good news? The promised paradise is presumably better than anything I know in this world. (There are jokes to be made here; perhaps the presence of certain husbands and certain wives could turn eternal life into a perfect hell.) Still, I find myself clinging to this life, full as it is of sorrows and joys. I find myself clinging to the smell of chlorine from my morning swim, to my favorite pop songs, to the sadnesses I have carried so long I don't know where they end and I begin. I find myself clinging to my husband.

I want him now, and I want him for eternity. Is that, after all, too much to ask?

15

THERE IS MERCY

The other day I was reading Sheldon Vanauken's memoir, *A Severe Mercy*, at the local swimming pool. I don't recommend this. There is a reason "beach reads" have sparkly pink covers and happy-go-lucky plotlines. When you are surrounded by masses of svelte suburban mothers, the paperback doubling as a rampart to conceal your bathing-suited stomach as you recline in a lounge chair should not move you to weep.

I'm not ruining anything by telling you Davy dies. You know from the preface that she will, and too young. You read the book to know why it is that her grief-stricken husband can claim that Davy's death is merciful—severely or otherwise.

I have a love-hate relationship with *A Severe Mercy*, which I first read in college at the behest of a cute boy. It's like a Nicholas Sparks novel for theology nerds: tragic and inspirational and soap operatic. Vanauken doesn't bother with illusions of modesty, and describes his book as "the spiritual autobiography of a love rather than the lovers." The plot is straightforward, sweeping through three acts. Act 1: Sheldon and Davy fall madly in love. They craft a relationship marked by remarkable intimacy; "total sharing, we felt, was the ultimate secret of a love that would last for ever."[1] They are determined that time will not test the mingling of their souls or tarnish the brilliance of their passion. Act 2: Sheldon and Davy, who married as self-avowed pagans, convert to Christianity with none other than Christian apologist and Oxford professor C. S. Lewis himself as a friend and mentor of the faith. And then the brutal third act: Davy up and dies of some mysterious illness she may or may not have contracted during their South Pacific sailboating days. Vanauken interprets her death as God's means of preserving their love and securing his faith. These are theological convictions of which I remain unconvinced.

But the painful conclusion of *A Severe Mercy* was not what made me fish for tissues at the pool. It was the story of a "cup of water in the night." When Sheldon and Davy were first establishing the commandments of their lifelong fling, they added courtesy to the canon. Along with total sharing, absolute courtesy would be a defense against the ravages of selfishness. "Whatever one of us asked the other to do—it was assumed the asker would weigh all consequences—the other would do. Thus one might wake the other in the night and ask for a cup of water; and the other would peacefully (and sleepily) fetch it."[2] A friend who also read the book in college told me that she found this completely ridiculous.

"Get your own water!" she exclaimed, bewildered by the planned mutual dependence.

Frankly, I don't recall reading that part as a single woman. It wouldn't have had any of the lush, romantic appeal of the couple's more obviously mesmerizing qualities. Why bother being aspirational about something as pedestrian as courtesy? I mentioned that Sheldon and Davy had a *yacht* and befriended *C. S. Lewis*, did I not? But courtesy—mutual, simple, profound—means a bit more to me than it did fifteen years ago, in part because my marriage has occasionally been a desert without a cup of water in the night to be found.

Here is where I should lead with a story of one of the many times I have been the discourteous culprit. But part of my problem is that I tend to most vividly remember the times it went the other way. We laugh about it now—what else could we do but laugh about it?—but I'll never forget when, not long after Juliette was born, I woke up in the middle of the night ravenously hungry. I had to nurse the squalling baby and could not quite bear the thought of waiting the forty minutes it took to feed her before I had a chance to feed myself. So I woke Benjamin up and asked him to bring me a toasted English muffin with peanut butter on it. I can still conjure the precise feeling of how desperately I wanted that snack; it's enough to make me want to pull a pair of pants on over my pajamas and run out to the supermarket for a sleeve of Thomas' English muffins this very moment.

Benjamin sleepily fetched my food. I actively pretended the great, heaving sigh he let out on the way to the kitchen was a tired yawn and not an irritated groan. When he presented the plate, my heart sank and my stomach growled: there was nowhere near enough peanut butter smeared on the muffin. I apologetically asked him to go back to the kitchen for more. At least, that's how I remember it—Benjamin would probably tell you I barked the command: *More peanut butter, now!* (He said, she said. I'm writing this book, so you get my version of the truth.)

However nicely or rudely the second request was delivered, I ended up with more peanut butter. Like, a lot more peanut butter. So much peanut butter that there was absolutely no possibility that it was anything other than a passive-aggressive amount of peanut butter. I wasn't about to send him back again for *less* peanut butter, so I ate it, all of it, one thick, stick-to-the-roof-of-your-mouth bite at a time.

I washed it down with a cup of water I fetched for myself.

I won't let myself off so easily, though, with my convenient amnesia about my own marital failings. Neither of us will soon forget the morning not long ago when I lost my temper at Benjamin at the neurology department of the local hospital. It's one thing to holler at your husband; it's another to holler at your husband while he is experiencing the blinding agony of a migraine headache.

We were there because his annual cluster headaches had done what we didn't think was even possible: they had gotten worse. I was terribly worried about my husband. To behold a loved one in pain is a harrowing thing. He was in so much pain that when the neurologist's assistant asked him what medications he was taking, he failed to mention the most important drug in our medical cabinet—his antidepressants, which had first been prescribed back in California. I piped up with the forgotten information, the picture of a helpful wife who was on top of her husband's health and wellness. But he insisted he was not presently taking any antidepressant medication.

This was news to me.

A courteous wife would have waited until his pain subsided. But as soon as we were out of earshot of the receptionist I dove right in, peppering Benjamin with questions about the Case of the Missing Serotonin Reuptake Inhibitors. As I ascertained that he had simply stopped taking his medication of his own volition, tears streamed down his face—partly due to the severity of his pain, and partly because when the migraines are at their worst, his bewildered sinuses tend to malfunction as well. And, no doubt, partly because his beloved spouse had metamorphosed into a livid shrew. And yet I seethed. I berated. I cursed. How could this man, who had suffered for years from undiagnosed and therefore untreated depression, decide to toss out the bottle of pills that was supposed to save him—and therefore me—from the depths of the illness? My fury evicted my empathy, especially as the inexplicably difficult preceding months became, all at once, explicable.

The fact is, just as Benjamin's capacity for courtesy had been frequently hampered by depression, his decision to stop taking his medication was itself a manifestation of the illness. When I finally stepped outside of myself long enough to realize this, I regained a modicum of lovingkindness toward the man with the monstrous migraine. Of course, by that time the headache was over. Not yet trusting myself to directly communicate with Benjamin about it without getting spitting mad again, I sent him a long text message. While he was recovering on the couch in the next room. (A well-timed text message has proven itself to be a handy instrument in our marital toolbox. The written word, even on a handheld device, seems to bring out the courtesy in us. At the very least, in text bubbles we can only YELL, not yell.) I did apologize for my poorly timed rant, but reiterated calmly what I had furiously sputtered an hour before: *You absolutely must make an appointment with your psychiatrist as soon as possible and promise me that you will not do this irresponsible thing again.*

In *A Severe Mercy*, the principles Sheldon and Davy set forth about intimacy and courtesy were all intended as a means to happily hide themselves behind a "Shining Barrier"—a metaphorical wall protecting them from anything that might detract from their love for one another. Depression is like that Shining Barrier, in a way. Or maybe it's precisely unlike the Shining Barrier. Rather than reflecting and magnifying light, it absorbs it like a fog. It suffocates joy, silences laughter, curtails aspiration. Like the lovers' shield, it does a swell job of wrapping itself around you, but it is less like a cocoon than a shroud. And there's no buddy system with depression. Its sharpest weapon is isolation. Depression can and does extinguish love—and, as we all know too well, it can even unmercifully extinguish life itself. For years, before Benjamin's depression was named, he was hidden from me behind its foggy barrier. He would emerge for days or weeks at a time, and I would rejoice at the uncharacteristic lightness in his step. But an insurmountable barrier marked by sullenness and insecurity and anger—the oft-unrecognized symptoms of depression in men—would invariably descend again, and I would once again wonder what the bloody heck was wrong with him.

This is why I lost my mind when my beloved all but dared the depression to return.

If there is a severe mercy in my marriage, it is not my husband's illness, but his diagnosis. Benjamin hated receiving the diagnosis; for him, rather than affirmation that the adversity wasn't his fault, it was confirmation that something in him was irreparably broken. He acutely felt that shame which so often accompanies matters of mental health. But I received the diagnosis as good news. To be sure, treating any mental illness is both a science and an art; it doesn't always respond to the available drugs as straightforwardly as, say, cholesterol cowers in the face of statins. But knowing the cause was, for me, cause for hope. He was the good man I knew him to be. The surly, distant, unpredictable man I lived with wasn't Benjamin; it was Depressed Benjamin. The dull barrier of depression had held the "real" Benjamin in thrall—and perhaps he could be returned to me.

There is mercy in Benjamin's absence every Tuesday night as he makes the long drive to spend an hour with his gifted therapist. There is mercy in the bottle of tiny capsules that sweep the fog away, mercy in Benjamin's affirmation that he will keep swallowing one each morning. (I daily pray for a related mercy: that the adjacent bottle of tiny capsules could keep those horrible migraines at bay.) There is mercy in being reunited not merely with the man I married, but with a man far more capable of joy than the man I married, a man who is restored not only to me, but also to himself. In the parables of Jesus, there is much rejoicing when that which was lost is found. This is a gladness I know firsthand, and it is this holy gladness—this profound thanksgiving to God, from whom all blessings flow—that is another of the gifts of our own severe mercy.

As for courtesy? Well. We're working on it. And although our love story bears little resemblance to that of Sheldon and Davy's, I am fully at peace with this. Their obsessive desire to maintain the heady passion and compassion of their earliest days as lovers is foreign to me. As much as I enjoyed our speedy courtship, ours is a relationship more akin to wine than fresh grapes. It's a cliché, but it's true: it gets better with age. It will not wither, and it will not rot. Each trial overcome, each wound healed, each imperfection embraced, each fight forgiven—they all, in good time, deepen our love far more than any shining but ultimately vulnerable fortress ever could.

16

THE HEM OF JOY'S GARMENT

I realize this is stating the obvious, but we are The Persheys. We are a unit, a team. Everyone except Benjamin and I are related by blood, and it shows: we all have the same outsized feelings, the same rowdy sense of humor, the same appetite for fun. There is a sweetness to our family life that all but undoes me. This household is the consequence of our marriage; these children, the proverbial fruit of our loins. We didn't build the house, but we made the home.

Dinnertime in our household is, like dinnertime in a lot of households, part sacred and part circus. I am the family cook. This is a role I have assumed not on account of any notable culinary skill but because I am the one with opinions about nutrition and a complex about food safety.

I start assembling the evening meal mere moments after kicking my clogs into the pile of shoes by the front door.

Quick, easy, and adaptable to the various taste preferences
to which I halfheartedly cater is the name of the game. In a
pinch, I serve up plates of whole wheat pasta with a generous
dusting of grated Parmesan for the girls—their current favorite—with the gourmet addition of canned puttanesca sauce
for the grownups. (Even if I didn't love puttanesca, I would
love puttanesca; thanks to a Marisa de los Santos novel, I
know that the tomato-based sauce is a "wee bit indecent . . .
for reasons best left obscure, 'puttanesca' derives from the
Italian word for 'whore.'" I never met a naughty etymology
I didn't love.) This pasta will be paired with the perennially
popular side of frozen peas, lovingly defrosted in the micro-
wave, or perhaps some oven-roasted asparagus if it is in season and I have the energy to face the inevitable backlash.

Sometimes we get testy with one another in the rush before
dinner—my mother always called that time the "witching
hour"—but after hands are washed, milk is poured, and the
matter of which child gets to drink from the prized blue jelly
glass is settled, we join hands and sing Johnny Appleseed.
*Oh, the Lord is good to me, and so I thank the Lord, for
giving me the things I need: the sun and the rain and the
appleseed. The Lord is good to me.* Every so often one of us
is still a sourpuss during the song, but generally speaking, this
ritual lifts our spirits even as it blesses our food. It's the grace
my family sang when I was a child, and even though I originally avoided introducing it in hopes that we would develop
a vocabulary of spoken prayer, the opening *Oh!* anchors me
in tradition even as it fills me with joy.

We eat together most nights, gathered around our
scratched-up, secondhand table that is shoved to the side of

the dining room to make room for our deceptively beautiful piano. Juliette's piano teacher tells us that it is one of the worst instruments he's ever encountered in all the years he's been showing up in parlors and living rooms to teach elementary school children. The surface of the piano is cluttered with stuff: framed snapshots, trinkets, preschool art, second-grade homework sheets. One of my favorite items is a small wooden carving of cats; a wheel can be spun to make the cats' heads turn toward one another and, inasmuch as wooden cats can, "kiss." When Benjamin gave it to me for Christmas the first year we were married, I was mystified. Needless to say, such a quirky tchotchke was not on my Christmas list. Now I cherish it with the full force of nostalgia.

Perched next to the cats is a print given to me by one of my oldest and dearest friends. It features a red bowtie superimposed over a page from the dictionary, stamped with the words "We're all stories in the end. Just make it a good one." It is one of those gifts that was precisely right; my friend knows that I love Doctor Who—from whence the quote comes—*especially* the particular incarnation of the Doctor character to which the bowtie perfectly references (#MattSmith). I love the notion that we are walking narratives, telling stories with our very lives (#DonaldMiller).

Dinnertime is storytelling time. As we eat, we take turns telling about our days. It's a variation of the Ignatian examen, a practice that encourages people to consider their daily consolations and desolations as a means of paying attention to the movement and direction of God. Rather than ask the more spiritually resonant "When were you most aware of God's presence?" we simply recount the best and worst parts of our days. Genevieve is a staunch believer that her role as the youngest in the family means she must always go first, so she might get things started by telling us about playing with our next-door neighbor Adam. Juliette frequently regales us with reports about recess, the perennial highlight of her young life. Benjamin might share a story about helping his clients find stable housing; though social work can be exhausting, the rare satisfaction of handing over house keys to a chronically homeless family makes up for his hard days at the support services center and long nights at the homeless shelter. If I've made it to a yoga class, I'm likely to name savasana as my favorite moment of the day—lately it seems as if I'm never not moving, so lying as still as a corpse is delightful.

As often as not, the girls respond that their favorite part of the day is "right now." I press for different answers; Benjamin and I treasure those precious reports from the hours we spend scattered across town. But my first response and truest answer is the same as theirs. The quotidian joy of eating with my family is hard to beat. On a recent night, we laughed until our sides hurt. I had found a gently used M&M's costume for Juliette to wear for Halloween, and she was scheming up complementary getups for the rest of us. "Genevieve is a Tootsie Roll, Mama is a Pershey Kiss, and—"

"And Daddy is a sucker!" Genevieve shouted with glee, blissfully ignorant of the double entendre.

With moments like these, I want to do what cannot be done: freeze the frame, stop the clock. I long to cling to the hem of joy's garment. Of course, nothing takes me out of a glorious "now" more effectively than worrying about when it will end. Brené Brown calls this phenomenon "foreboding joy"—the fear of losing the very thing that gives you pleasure.

Louis C. K. has a bit called "Countdown to Sorrow" that is, more or less, a comedian's take on foreboding joy. "Everything that makes you happy is going to end," he says, and provides proof for his theory: puppies. Bringing home a puppy might seem like cause for gladness, but what you're really saying is this: "Hey look, everyone, we're all going to cry soon!"[1] He says it for laughs, but it's more sad than funny. And it's true. You might get a decade, give or take a few years, before you're crouched and bawling on a tile floor while a veterinarian quietly injects a fatal dose of barbiturates into the hind leg of the dog-that-used-to-be-a-puppy on your lap. But must we consider the end, even at the beginning? Must our future grief eclipse our present gift, the inevitability of sorrow eclipse the moment of joy?

I suspect the antidote to this conundrum is the wisdom of 1 Thessalonians: "Rejoice always, pray without ceasing, give thanks in all circumstances; for this is the will of God in Christ Jesus for you" (5:16-18). To say that "rejoicing always" is not my forte is an understatement. I excel at the art of lamentation—that is, the spiritual discipline of agonizing. Giving thanks in the face of pain, loss, or Monday mornings is not in my nature.

Not long ago Genevieve pitched an extraordinary fit during dinner. She wanted Parmesan dusted on her macaroni and cheese, and Benjamin nixed the request. Personally, I would not have chosen to fight this particular battle, but we try to refrain from undermining each other's parenting decisions in front of the girls. Even if I had crossed him, I am loathe to give in to the demands of a tantruming child. I inwardly fumed that we had to eat our meal to the soundtrack of needless screaming. I suggested to Genevieve that she could tell us the best part of her day once she had calmed down. With tears still rolling down her cheeks and a sob caught in her throat, she pouted, "Right now."

Benjamin and I exchanged incredulous looks. I reminded Genevieve that she had, in fact, *gone to a birthday party at Chuck E. Cheese's that very morning.* She repeated her answer in an indignant screech. "Right now!" We couldn't conceal our laughter. Even Genevieve joined in. Maybe she was merely proud of herself for unexpectedly evoking our positive attention. Maybe she too noted the irony. She was miserable, by all objective measures, yet stubbornly insisted that dinner with her family trumped arcade games with her friends. It was the oddest example of "giving thanks in all circumstances" I've ever encountered, but it's stuck with me.

I have a friend with four young daughters, including twin babies who were altogether unplanned. Christen and her husband love their children desperately. But they do not necessarily enjoy this chapter of their story, which includes three kids in diapers. They are clinging not to daily joy, but to expectant hope—that they will survive this season with their sanity and their marriage intact. Christen recently confided that an old friend of hers had recently divorced her husband, not long after the couple's youngest child graduated from college. This particular story arc—the empty-nest divorce—is all too common. Couples, consciously or otherwise, often hold it together for the children's sake, parting ways as soon as the children are children no more. Christen told her husband the news of their friend in their minivan on the way home from a disastrous outing. The girls were squabbling in the backseat; as usual, one kid was caterwauling. "Let's stay married long enough so we can enjoy what comes next together," Christen said to her husband. They both smiled, imagining some distant time in the future when they would again have date night, and maybe even no minivan. Not long ago she ordered custom throw pillows for their basement sofa. One is embroidered with the word *clowns*, the other with *jokers*. She and her husband sit between those pillows—clowns on the left, jokers to the right—while the kids run circles around them. They chuckle at their own cleverness: they are most definitely stuck in the middle. Of their chaos, and of their story. Even as they are eager to drastically reduce the amount of conjunctivitis and Kidz Bop they must regularly withstand together, they are doing their best to rejoice, and give thanks. Even to laugh.

As for Benjamin and me, we are in what feels like a nearly perfect middle: free of both infant diapers and preteen drama. The marriage is more solid than our 1929 hardwood floors (the plumber just apologetically informed me that our bathroom floorboards have rotted out and will need to be replaced). The children still show up in our bed most nights in search of warm snuggles, but they rarely wake us up as they slip under the covers. Even in this sweet spot, we have our fair share of lousy moments and rotten days. I am learning to see the rough patches as poignant in their own way; through them, we learn the ways of love and forgiveness and forbearance.

Not long ago, our church hosted a marriage enrichment retreat led by the popular blogger and psychologist Kelly Flanagan and his wife, who is also named Kelly Flanagan and who is also a psychologist. The Kelly Flanagans guided the participants through a series of conversations in which couples identified turning points, values, and future intentions. We surprised ourselves by spending a significant amount of time talking about our first dog, Deacon. We adopted Deacon within weeks of moving from student housing to our parsonage near the beach; the pit bull mix accompanied me to the office during my early days as a pastor. He was a great dog: docile, loyal, playful. We took him on long walks twice a day, usually together. He was diagnosed with lymphoma and died just a little more than a year after we adopted him.

Deacon's leash was a lifeline, and the loss undid me. I was still so new to pastoral ministry. We were still so lousy at loving one another. We tried and failed to adopt another dog, but there was no replacing Deacon. A decade later, we recalled that dog as absolutely critical to our marriage. We wept all over again, remembering our brief time with him with awe and thanksgiving.

So, yes, the puppy portends sorrow. "Right now" isn't always roses—in fact, it usually isn't roses. But even a family's sorrows give can give way to gratitude, eventually. I suspect opening ourselves to receive the gifts and the griefs of each chapter as it unfolds is the key to making our story a good one. Together.

17

WHEN JUSTICE ROLLS DOWN

I am living a life that is so good I am almost embarrassed by it. My family lives in a small, sturdy Dutch Colonial house with a new roof and a thirty-year mortgage. It is charming, as are the lilacs lining our driveway. You should not be at all surprised that I recently called a local contractor about getting an estimate for a white picket fence. We lack the half a kid in the two-point-five kids scenario of the American dream, but otherwise, we pretty much fit the bill.

I frequently cite the role of God's grace in redeeming my marriage, but the truth is that we have benefited not only from blessing, but also from privilege.

I am sheepish about this privilege. No matter that we have a bit of debt (the "good" kind) and all share one tiny bathroom; we have slipped through the back door and into the upper middle class. All the benefits and pitfalls of affluence are ours to explore. I vaguely recall a younger version of myself, the one who chose her seminary based on the reputation of its urban ministry program, the one who protested war in the streets of Los Angeles. Nowadays cities unnerve me, and I prefer to be happily ensconced in the suburbs. While I was discerning if God was calling me to this community, one of the few concerns I had was the comfort of the life I might lead here. Several people reminded me that affluent communities need help, too. This is true. Affluent communities sometimes need *more* help, for the brokenness concealed behind a charming façade can be even harder to heal than the brokenness on display. But it is also true that living in a quaint village and serving a handsomely resourced church is generally pleasant.

I went to graduate school to study theology in the early 2000s, and the first of many things that blew my mind was being directed to write my papers in the first person. Until that point in my formal education, "I" was unwelcome in academic writing. "I" was for your diary and your love letters, not your critical analysis of Shakespeare's *Othello*. But during the first week of seminary I was introduced to the concept of social location. At the start of my essays, I was to locate myself and my identity. The point was to establish a context for whatever argument that followed, to acknowledge that my take on the topic at hand was inescapably influenced by my race, my class, my gender. No single voice got to be authoritative; everyone had a social location—even the straight, white European men whose systematic theologies still made up the greater part of our curriculum.

These days, an awareness of social location, particularly as it relates to racial and economic privilege, has spread far beyond the ivory tower. While the practice of naming privilege is still controversial in some circles, more people are acknowledging that identity affords certain advantages and disadvantages. Without a doubt, this book is profoundly shaped by my social location—by the particularly pleasant field in which I make my notes and observations. My experience of and observations about marriage are not universal. They are colored by my perspective as a white, educated, (upper-ish) middle-class, cisgender, heterosexual woman who was raised by long-married parents.

While my own marriage closely adheres to the cultural norm, I am glad that there are more ways than ever to be a family these days. I am glad for a single friend who conceived her beloved daughter by way of donor sperm, glad for gay friends who fostered-to-adopt, glad for child-free friends who are pleased as punch with their families of two. This is not to say I am unconcerned that there are so many more children being raised by parents who are not bound together by the covenant of marriage. Healthy two-parent households do contribute to the well-being of children. Despite the high value I place on marriage, I count it a blessing that unwed mothers are no longer shamed as a matter of course. It is an unequivocally good thing that the children of unmarried parents are no longer branded "illegitimate" (which, like "illegal," strikes me as an adjective that should never be used to describe a human being who was fearfully and wonderfully made).

For all the trends worthy of celebration, there are also trends that merit concern. There is a great deal of dysfunction and disorder affecting American families—and this dysfunction and disorder is disproportionately affecting American families that are poor and nonwhite.

Divorce rates, as well as marriage and out-of-wedlock childbirth rates, vary widely when broken down by demographics. In *Just Married: Same-Sex Couples, Monogamy, and the Future of Marriage*, Stephen Macedo addresses the extraordinary inequity. He notes the significant disparities that crop up between people who have only a high school education and those who have earned a college degree. The gap is in part economic: well-paying jobs for people who do not have at least an associate's degree are few and far between. This gap also manifests itself in marriage: for couples who both have college degrees, Macedo notes, "divorce rates have declined to the levels of the mid-1960s."[1]

As of a few years ago, when Benjamin completed his college degree, my own marriage is officially near the top of the socioeconomic ladder. Though I know this is merely anecdotal and probably the consequence of any number of factors, a significant turning point in our marriage was, in fact, his graduation. Our financial strain lessened considerably as he became eligible for higher-paying jobs. There was an emotional impact as well. Now that he was no longer a "college dropout," the sore spot in Benjamin's ego healed.

Macedo points out that for those with less education and economic stability, as well as for African Americans, the rate of divorce remains quite steep. He becomes a scholarly harbinger of doom: "Because marriage does confer benefits on children, financially, emotionally, and in terms of cognitive development, this class divide within marriage suggests that class divisions in our society will grow worse in the decades ahead."[2]

For Christians inclined to care about matters of justice, these are profoundly sobering observations. Sociologists and policymakers have long been alarmed by the decline in marriage rates and the rise of divorce. In 2001, George W. Bush's administration passed the Healthy Marriage Initiative (HMI), through which roughly $1.5 billion was earmarked to promote marriage, primarily through advertising campaigns and educational opportunities for low-income couples.[3] The effectiveness of the programs was mixed; while participants reported "slightly less" abuse and psychological distress, "the program did not significantly affect whether couples stayed married at the 12-month follow-up point."[4] Critics who doubted all along that the government could or even should fix intimate relationships were none too fond of the HMI. Whatever good the federal government has done to support marriage, many argue that it has done far more to sabotage marriage, particularly for the most economically disadvantaged. People who receive welfare benefits are at risk of losing them if they marry; all the pro-marriage propaganda in the world won't convince a couple to put a ring on it if it means risking the government assistance that puts food on the table and medicine in the cabinet.

Like Macedo, sociologist Andrew Cherlin comments on the decline of marriage within black communities. "At current rates, only about two out of three black women will marry during their lifetimes. And their marriages are very

fragile: 70 percent are projected to end in divorce or separation, a much higher percentage than among whites (47
percent)."[5] This is a grievous, heartbreaking disparity.

I wanted to learn more about marriage in African American communities from an African American scholar, rather
than relying solely on the observations of white writers. My
search let me to a book by Ralph Richard Banks, a married
black man who teaches at Stanford Law School. The title—
Is Marriage for White People?—caused my mother no small
amount of self-consciousness when I sent her to the library
on a mission to pick up my interlibrary loan copy. The title
references a claim made by a black sixth-grade boy—a boy
clearly growing up in a context in which strong marriages
were lamentably absent.

Banks integrates sociological research with a series of
interviews with black women, a powerful means of humaniz-
ing what might otherwise become disembodied statistics. He
acknowledges two traditional explanations for the state of
black marriage. The first, obviously, is slavery.[6] Slavery trau-
matized black people in every imaginable way—or, truly, in
every unimaginable way. One of its most ruinous legacies was
the annihilation of healthy marriage and family relationships.
White men raped black women. Children were sold to other
masters. Black fathers were separated from their partners and
their children alike. Some claim that slavery was abolished
too long ago to have ongoing consequences for marriage and
family life, but black people were enslaved in this country far
longer than they have been free. Indeed, it won't be until the
futuristic-sounding year 2111 that the era of freedom will
have been as long as the era of slavery.

Banks also considers the role of African culture in shaping contemporary black families, in which extended familial relationships are frequently vibrant. "The idea here is that the African societies from which the slaves were taken featured extended family structures in which marriage was less pivotal."[7] (I remember my amazement upon learning that my black friends nearly all had close relationships with their cousins. I wouldn't even recognize my first cousins on the street.) Black children raised by a team of mothers, aunts, and grandmothers can experience the loving stability and security that many associate only with two-parent households.

Banks believes that both the effects of slavery on gender relations and the influence of African culture are insufficient explanations for the low rates of marriage at every socioeconomic rung of the black community. He considers a constellation of factors that contribute to the crisis, from the astonishingly high incarceration rate for black men to the widening educational and economic inequality between black men and black women. With significant numbers of poorer black men considered unsuitable for marriage due to underemployment, drug use, and criminal records, and many middle-class black men pursuing interracial marriage, there is, according to Banks, an imbalanced "market" for potential mates. The dearth of "marriageable" men forces many black women to either marry "down"—establishing relationships that are frequently unstable—or to simply remain single, even if that means taking on sole parenting responsibilities. (It bears mentioning that Banks's book, which ultimately puts forth the partial solution that more black women should marry white men to even out the playing field, has a mixed reception in the black community.)

Some years ago I met the Rev. Theresa S. Thames at a ministry conference, and I've been grateful to carry on the friendship through social media, where I am continually educated and inspired by her words about theology, culture, race, and marriage.[8] Not long ago she posted something that led me to believe that she might well have a lot to say about marriage in the black community, and she did indeed.

Theresa's painful marriage and divorce were deeply affected by powers and principalities beyond their immediate relationship. "As an educated Black woman who married an educated Black man," she explained to me in an email, "there was still this competition factory of 'success' and 'winning' that made marriage difficult. We were working so hard to *avoid* the negative stereotype of Black marriages that we were living right into it." While her ex-husband's infidelities were the catalyst for their divorce, Theresa acknowledges that their problems started even before they were married—truly, long before they were born. Unlike Banks, she points to slavery as the crack in the foundation of black families. Whereas Banks claims that slavery was too long ago to continue to have an impact on intimate relationships, Theresa's reflections imply that the effects of what some call "America's original sin" accrue; they are multiplied exponentially over generations, and are fueled by ongoing systemic racism and bias. "Very little in American society has ever championed and fully supported the holistic nature, development, and love of Black marriages," she declared.

Unfortunately, even one of the institutions in American society that is of central significance to Theresa failed her: the church. The marriage counseling her pastor provided was shamefully inadequate. "We did no work around family of origin, core values, goals, personal intimate needs, etc.," she reflected. "It was basically a packet of photocopied questions based on biblical ideas of marriage regarding honoring, cleaving, obeying. We were given this package to complete and discuss, that was it. The church marries people and then throws them into the pool to 'figure it out' on their own." Theresa herself is a gifted pastor, and is an incisive practical theologian and cultural commentator. She recently wrote on social media, "The Christian church really does a poor job of supporting marriage. Let's be real about the misogynistic and emotionally abusive theology that is preached from pulpits, shared in Bible studies, and given in marriage counseling sessions." Theresa actively works to challenge this theology and change the narrative about marriage in the black community. This is work she is uniquely qualified to undertake; she is a "wounded healer," to borrow the language of Carl Jung and Henri Nouwen.

As for me, I am humbled. I used to crack this totally *hilarious* joke that paying a housecleaner to deal with our grody kitchen counters was a lot cheaper than marriage counseling, and often just as effective at resolving simmering conflicts. Now I cringe at my insensitivity and the ease with which I wielded my economic privilege. It doesn't feel comfortable to realize how much of one's experience is dictated by race and class; I suspect this is why folks get defensive when the subject comes up.

Acknowledging the ways privilege has cushioned our marriage doesn't detract from what we've put into it. All the wealth and white privilege in the world can't make up for meager commitment or a lack of love, and to be sure, many black marriages are resilient, loving, and lifelong. (I am this close to adding a framed photo of the Obamas to the gallery wall on our stairwell, so charmed am I by Barack and Michelle's mutual affection and respect. They could be the poster couple for #VeryMarried.) But as my understanding deepens of the ways that socioeconomic disadvantage contributes to the decline in marriage, I am ever more suspicious of easy answers and pat solutions. Much as the pro-life movement is only as strong as its commitment to promoting the welfare of mothers and children, the pro-marriage movement is only as effective as its commitment to pursuing economic and social justice.

If we want to wax poetic about the virtues and benefits of marriage, we must also advocate for policies and programs that empower people to access those virtues and benefits for themselves. "Family values"—a politically loaded phrase if there ever was one—needs to be radically enlarged to include prison reform, education reform, and increased economic opportunity.

Marriages will be stronger when justice rolls down like waters, and righteousness like an ever-flowing stream.

18

YOKED TO ANOTHER FAMILY

Once upon a time, a man named Jacob met a woman named Rachel at a well. Rachel was a shepherd who kept her father's sheep, and Jacob was her first cousin. According to the cultural mores of their day, this was beneficial, not detrimental, to their case as potential mates.

Their first encounter was dramatic; Jacob helped water Rachel's sheep, kissed her, and wept. Laban—Rachel's father, Jacob's uncle—ran out to meet his long-lost nephew, hugging and kissing him and bringing him into the care and protection of his home. The men brokered a deal: Jacob would serve Laban for seven years to earn the honor of marrying Rachel. Though younger than her doe-eyed sister, Leah, Rachel was beautiful. "So Jacob served seven years for Rachel," Genesis tells us, "and they seemed to him but a few days because of the love he had for her" (Genesis 29:20). But it turned out Uncle Laban had a nefarious streak; after serving his time and spending the night with his bride, "Rachel," Jacob discovered in the morning that Laban had sent Leah, not Rachel, to consummate the marriage. "This is not done in our country," Laban explained, "giving the younger before the firstborn" (Genesis 29:26).

You might have mentioned that seven years ago, sir.

Laban let Jacob marry Rachel the next week—but not before making Jacob promise him seven *more* years of labor in exchange for his second daughter. After several years and a telenovela's worth of drama, Jacob vacated his father-in-law's household in a hurry, taking off with his wives, children, and his shadily appropriated livestock. Laban caught up to Jacob, and the men had a testy exchange about some missing household gods. Unbeknownst to Jacob, his beloved Rachel had, in fact, secreted them away in the saddle of her camel. Jacob and Laban hashed it out and parted ways, but not without making a covenant: "Then Laban said to Jacob, 'See this heap and see the pillar, which I have set between you and me. This heap is a witness, and the pillar is a witness, that I will not pass beyond this heap to you, and you will not pass beyond this heap and this pillar to me, for harm'" (Genesis 31:51-52).

I know a few people who could use a heap, a pillar, and a holy vow marking the boundary between them and their inlaws.

The epic fiasco that unfolded between Jacob and Laban isn't even the most dysfunctional of biblical inlaw relations.

I am fairly sure that dubious honor goes to Tamar's experience of marrying into Judah's family tree. When her marriage to Judah's son Er ended with her untimely entrance into widowhood—God struck Er down because Er was so wicked—Tamar was married off to Er's younger brother Onan. This was in accordance with Levirate marital customs that protected women in the patriarchal society by ensuring they would still have a place in their husbands' families. (Oh, biblical marriage. How you thwart the presumptions and chuckle in the face of Western definitions of "family values"!)

Onan didn't want to sustain the economic blow of giving Tamar an heir, so he "spilled his seed" to avoid impregnating her. This is, of course, the origin of *onanism*, and Onan's failure to honor his responsibility to his sister-in-law/wife resulted in him, too, being struck dead by God. (We can contemplate the theology of divine capital punishment another time, okay?)

At this point in the saga, Judah was beginning to suspect that Tamar was at fault; there was an uncomfortable correlation between his sons marrying Tamar and meeting their demise. Someone really needed to explain to this man that correlation does not necessarily mean causation! Judah would not let his youngest son marry his seemingly fatal daughter-in-law, even though it was mandatory according to the stipulations of Levirate law. Intrepid Tamar took matters into her own hands. She disguised herself as a prostitute and convinced Judah to avail himself of her services. Impregnated by her own father-in-law, Tamar was clever enough to procure incontrovertible proof that she was to bear the heir of

Judah. Perez, son of Tamar and Judah, is listed in the ancestry of Jesus at the beginning of the gospel of Matthew.

Not all biblical inlaw relationships are marred by deceit, dishonesty, violence, and entrapment-by-prostitution. There is, of course, the shining example of Ruth and her mother-in-law, Naomi. Ruth, a Moabite, could have returned to her own kindred after the death of her husband. But she pledged her commitment to Naomi in a poignant oath:

> Do not press me to leave you
> or to turn back from following you!
> Where you go, I will go;
> where you lodge, I will lodge;
> your people shall be my people,
> and your God my God.
> Where you die, I will die—
> there will I be buried.
> May the Lord do thus and so to me,
> and more as well,
> if even death parts me from you! (Ruth 1:16b-17)

In a culture that frequently demonizes relationships between mothers- and daughters-in-law, it is remarkable that this text is so frequently recited during weddings. I guess everyone accepts the false pretense that it is a vow between two lovers, not a vow between a daughter-in-law and her deceased husband's mother. I would love to see the *Knot* or *Vogue Weddings* publish a cover story on the original contexts of popular wedding Scriptures.

This is where you should find a candid exploration of the triumphs and torments of inlaw relationships that make up my family tree. However, candidness doesn't always go over well at the Thanksgiving feast, does it? Tact and discretion and not writing your mother-in-law into your marriage memoir all tend to be best practices in this particular dimension of married life.

The truth is, there is a great deal of mutual respect and affection between all the relevant parties. Benjamin loves my parents, and they love him. It is a family joke that he is the favorite son-in-law on account of his willingness to call my mother Mama, as my sisters and I do. My brothers-in-law don't call her anything, and I'm fairly sure they both still think of my father as Mr. Willis, which is natural, considering both of my sisters married their high school sweethearts.

I love Benjamin's mother, and father, and stepmother, and if they harbor suspicions about my character or devotion to their son, they hide them very well. I get to be an aunt to a few lovely children to whom I am not related by blood, and Benjamin is a beloved uncle to my sisters' children. There have been bumps along the way, to be sure. It is hard enough to handle one's own family; when you marry, you are suddenly related to a family governed by a wholly foreign internal logic, yoked by a history to which you are privy only secondhand, and that may have an entirely different idea of what constitutes a proper chocolate chip cookie. There is a reason inlaws have a reputation as, well, *out*laws. The whole scene can be quite the sticky wicket.

Much of the literature about managing inlaw relationships focuses on the necessity for spouses to "leave and cleave"—a reference to the Genesis bit about how "a man leaves his father and his mother and clings to his wife, and they become one flesh" (Genesis 2:24). Leaning too heavily on one's parents and too lightly on one's spouse can no doubt be an issue, as can giving free rein to interfering inlaws. Establishing that your present family takes some precedence over your family of origin is good and right, if tricky.

But family of origin retains considerable sway, always and ever. In her book *Is Everyone Hanging Out Without Me?*, Mindy Kaling writes, "All a girl wants to do is to get along with her family and if you are on the side of making it easy, you will be loved eternally. It might be easier to condemn them—especially if she's doing that already—but, remarkably, even if they are murderers, she will find the good in them, especially if you start trashing them."[1] This is sound advice, I think, and how Benjamin and I have, intentionally or not, approached one another's families. I think Benjamin's relationships with his kin are stronger because of my presence and participation in his family, and I know my relationships with my parents and sisters are stronger because of his presence and participation in mine.

The role of inlaw networks is truncated from what it's been for much of history; one of the reasons people today have more autonomy to marry whom they wish is because their parents' fortunes aren't dependent on dowries and dynasties. Even without such consequential social and economic implications, the personal implications of marriage on families is incalculable. When Benjamin and I got engaged, I looked forward to meeting his extended family and knew, on a purely theoretical level, that they would become my family as well. Say, hypothetically speaking, they had been a disaster. I could have decided that I didn't want to marry Benjamin enough to put up with his family. But his family? They had no choice in the matter. If they didn't like me, there was nothing they could do about it. Sure, they could plead their case with Benjamin. They could exclude us from holiday gatherings. But they were powerless to prevent me from becoming legally connected to their family.

As it is, they didn't approach our nuptials with any obstructionism whatsoever; they welcomed me warmly. Still, my presence at family gatherings was disruptive—not in a negative connotation of the word, but in the literal sense that my presence changed the way things had been before. They weren't necessarily used to someone who, for instance, spends hours reading on vacation, or who gives hand-knit Christmas gifts, or who couldn't care less about football. Through the years, though, I've become a full member of Benjamin's family, and he of mine—relationships sealed not only by legalities but also by love.

For the past couple of summers, my mother-in-law has come to live with us for the summer to help care for our children while they are out of school. During the weeks before her first summer with us, I was nervous—and not only because we have one bathroom and there's often a line for the john with just the four of us. When I told friends about our plans, I could see their eyes widen as they imagined their own mothers-in-law moving in on a semipermanent basis. By the time she descended the escalator at Chicago Midway, I'd second-guessed the whole plan.

But it turned out wonderfully. She cooked and cleaned and played with the girls and basically made life easier in every possible way. Benjamin had extended time with his mother for the first time in his adulthood. (We'll consider those years he lived with her in his early twenties "pre-adulthood.") The girls got to know the grandmother who has lived half a country away from them for their entire lives. I had someone to take to the Indian food buffet and, even more importantly, someone who understood firsthand the delights and frustrations of living with a certain redhead.

I count down the days until my mother-in-law returns each summer.

Really.

19

SUBJECT TO ONE ANOTHER

I used to be Katherine Elaine Willis. When Benjamin and I married, I wanted the best of both worlds: a feminist retention of the name I'd had all my life, and a new name that rhymed with a brand of chocolate, didn't start with the fourth-to-last letter of the alphabet, and symbolized that we were family.

My intended did offer to become a Willis, but I didn't take him up on it. Pershey is an exceedingly rare name—so rare, in fact, that we are related in some way to virtually everyone who has it. I took the name gratefully, receiving it as I would a wedding gift from my groom. Once, at the local pool, I noticed a fabulous tattoo artfully inked on the foot of an otherwise straight-laced suburban mom: "There was nothing worth sharing like the love that let us share our name." When I saw it, I thought: Yep, *that* is why I am a Pershey, why I

absolutely must share a name with not only my children, but
also my husband. (Upon Googling the phrase, I found that
it's a line from an Avett Brothers song, which I have proceeded to listen to obsessively.) I know the practice of wives
taking their husband's surnames is a patriarchal tradition,
and I respect why many women chose not to. For me, the
symbol of sharing a name is more potent than the attending
patriarchal implications.

The name conundrum was the first of many invitations to
consider the ways that gender might inform the practicalities
of our marriage. We've ended up with a hodgepodge of traditional and nontraditional roles, mainly because we decided
a long time ago to do what worked best for our household
and not be beholden to cultural norms about which spouse
should do what. Benjamin supported us financially when I
was in graduate school; now I'm the primary breadwinner.
He stayed home with the girls when they were babies, but
is also the designated spider killer and trash taker-outer. He
does nearly all the literal driving, but I tend to be the one in
the metaphorical driver's seat of our family life. This works
for us.

We are, in the theological parlance of the day, in an "egalitarian" marriage of equals, as opposed to a "complementarian" marriage, which prescribes different roles and responsibilities to partners based on their respective genders. I suspect
most liberal mainline Christians tend to not even consider
the possibility of hierarchical marriage. I confirmed my
theory by polling a group of progressive clergy colleagues;
one noted that *complementarian* and *egalitarian* were not
"words I ever really think of in terms of marriage, mine or

anybody else's—though I know other people do. We always just assumed we would be equal partners in this; I don't think I realized there was another choice. And I certainly wouldn't have entertained a potential spouse who would have thought otherwise." Indeed, my liberal Christian friends are, by and large, less concerned about biblical gender norms than about the ways that sexism and toxic messages about masculinity compromise the health and well-being of relationships and individuals (cough, cough, Mark Driscoll).

Despite my evangelical leanings, I am culturally and theologically pretty solidly mainline. Fun fact: until I started paying more attention to the way marriage is discussed within more conservative circles, I had never even heard the word *complementarian* used in a sentence, let alone a sermon. Yet passages such as Paul's words about marriage in his letter to the Ephesians are, for many theologically and culturally conservative Christian communities, central to the conversation about marriage. They are not at all central to the way marriage is understood in progressive mainline congregations such as mine. But here's the thing: I believe that as Christians, we must take the Bible seriously. Not literally, mind you. But *seriously*. Ignoring texts such as Paul's Ephesians letter does a disservice to the community of faith. One cannot faithfully contemplate marriage from a Christian perspective without addressing the reality that some biblical texts do seem to promote hierarchy in marriage. Newly convicted of this, not long ago I did something entirely out of character. Something altogether unexpected. I preached on Ephesians 5:21-33.

The Scripture starts safely enough: "Be subject to one another out of reverence for Christ." But in the next breath, it dives into territory that is pretty foreign to a congregation affiliated with the theologically and culturally progressive United Church of Christ. "Wives, be subject to your husbands as you are to the Lord. For the husband is the head of the wife just as Christ is the head of the church, the body of which he is the Savior."

Although Christians theoretically consider the whole Bible holy and worthy of our attention, most of us are selective about which biblical passages we allow to be authoritative in our lives. Of course, most of us roundly deny this practice, which doesn't make it any less rampant. As for my own colleagues and parishioners who avoid texts such as this one from Ephesians, there's a general consensus that Paul's writings emerged from a profoundly different context from our own, and that his ideas about gender don't necessarily hold in the contemporary world. It's quite possible that it had been fifty years since this text was read from the pulpit in my church.

So I shouldn't have been surprised that, as I stood in the pulpit with my dangly earrings and clergy vestments and opened my mouth to read a text that has been used to subjugate women, an alto in the chancel choir would loudly react. "Just as the church is subject to Christ, so also wives ought to be, in everything, to their husbands," I read.

"Harrumph!" exclaimed the alto, sort of but not quite like one might interject a biblical reading with a reverent "Mm-hmm. Amen!" It was loud enough to be heard by everyone in the chancel.

It was a moment before I could regain my composure to complete the reading. Complementarian theologians would have been deeply offended. Of course, they likely would have been deeply offended by the mere presence of a female preacher, and would have walked out long before the feminist exclamation.

I remember hearing that same Ephesians passage read from a pulpit precisely once in my life. I was at my friend Twyla's wedding, just a few weeks before my own wedding day. As the minister of her conservative Baptist congregation began to speak of wives submitting to husbands, my friend Lorelei, seated in the pew next to me, grabbed my arm.

The minister went on to explain to the bride and groom the hierarchy that would forevermore structure their marriage—the roles that would govern their relationship. As the husband, Lucas would be the head of their household. He would make the decisions. He would report directly to Christ. As the wife, Twyla would submit to Lucas's spiritual and practical leadership. She would report directly to Lucas. She would accept his authority in their house and in her life. By the time the pastor concluded his wedding homily, my flesh was marked with a constellation of half-moons. Lorelei had taken her feminist fury out on my arm with her fingernails.

On the drive to the reception hall, we soberly debriefed the wedding. Twyla had always been one of our brightest and most grounded friends. She was independent, confident, and talented. She transcended the boy craziness that marked so many of our peers, myself included. Lorelei's eyes filled with tears. Her anger had given way to anguish. "I feel like Twyla just willingly subsumed her whole existence to a *boy*."

At the time, I fully agreed with Lorelei's assessment. I grieved the presence of an oppressive teaching in the sacred text of my own religion. I was a Christian and a woman, but I wasn't *that* kind of Christian woman. I had no intention of becoming that kind of Christian wife.

I still find that pastor's application of the text problematic. I must admit, however, that my assumptions about Twyla did not pan out. Even though Twyla willingly entered a marriage of what I consider intentional inequality, she never stopped being bright, grounded, independent, confident, and talented. She seems—from the outside looking in, anyway—to be quite happily married. And Twyla is not the only woman I know who interprets the Bible this way who has disrupted my assumptions. These friends have forced me to acknowledge that theologically and culturally conservative Christianity does not necessarily make for oppressed and downtrodden women. Indeed, some studies indicate that women in egalitarian marriages are *less* happy than women in complementarian marriages.[1]

To be sure, this isn't to say that women in hierarchical marriages are never oppressed and downtrodden. Sexism is a real problem, in both the public and the private sphere. When religion is used to justify oppression of any stripe, people of faith should speak out.

The irony is this: In its original context, this text was intended not to subjugate women, but to raise them up. Paul was writing, as we know, to the community in Ephesus, a Greek city. Women in ancient Greece did not have an abundance of human rights; they were not considered equal to men. As backward as this text might sound to contemporary ears, it was in fact pretty progressive in its original context. It's easy to get stuck on the part about wives being subject to husbands, but the passage does begin, "Be subject to one another out of reverence for Christ." This implies a mutuality in marriage that was entirely out of step with the mores of ancient Greek society. Given that wives were essentially the property of their husbands, it was no small thing that Paul encouraged men to love their wives.

As Sarah Bessey notes in her book *Jesus Feminist*, "These passages were actually subversive in their time because they placed demands on the assumed power of men (teaching them to be kind to their slaves, to be gentle with their children, to love their wives) and because they addressed the most powerless in a patriarchal society—the women, the children, the slaves."[2] I've noticed that many Christians struggle to give Paul the benefit of the doubt. He is indeed a complicated and occasionally maddening architect of early Christian thought. But if you can bear to suspend your misgivings about Paul, there is truly good news in his writings, and not only for the Christians of ancient Ephesus. For us. Remember that this is, after all, the same Paul who proclaimed that "there is no longer male and female; for all of you are one in Christ Jesus" (Galatians 3:28).

In the *Women's Bible Commentary* published by the evangelical-leaning InterVarsity Press, Claire M. Powell pushes back against hierarchical interpretations of this text and offers rich alternative readings. She considers what it truly means to "be subject." She understands submission as "not something enforced but embraced voluntarily, out of love for Christ and for one another."[3] Powell suggests that "another way of thinking of it may be giving in. Giving in to others or compromising our needs or wishes is something that is necessary to make a relationship work and is eventually a mark of strength, not of weakness. The relationship advocated is not one of doormat to exploiter but of equals giving in at appropriate times to each other in love."[4] That sounds to me like a pretty great relationship.

Powell goes on to ponder what Paul might have meant when he argued that "the husband is the head of the wife just as Christ is the head of the church." She notes that the word *head* often carries the connotation of ruler or boss, but that Paul's emphasis here is not on the "glorious ruling of Christ but of his self-giving sacrifice. . . . What the husband stands for when described as head is the caring, giving, sacrificial love that is like Christ."[5] In turn, wives are encouraged to love their husbands with the same caliber of devotion the church confers upon Christ. It is not a matter of who's in charge, or who has the power. It is a metaphor: for mutuality, for love, for devotion.

We throw out the baby with the bathwater if we write off Paul as outmoded and irrelevant. Part of what we lose, if we neglect the wisdom of this tricky text, is the "great mystery," the profound parallel Paul sets forth: the relationship between spouses is an echo of the relationship between Christ and the church. (Way to raise the stakes, Paul.)

I think of a friend who is half a generation or so older than I am, who has been married nearly twice as long as Benjamin and I. She recently divulged that her marriage has been fragile for some years, and that recently the latent issues imploded. She had always been, she explained, beholden to fairly traditional gender roles within her marriage, probably as much on account of cultural influences as spiritual ones. Her instinct was to submit, to serve, to subsume her own happiness to that of her husband's. All at once she realized how very unhappy she had become, and how much more she was pouring into their relationship than he was. The give was all hers; the take, his. She ended up seeking out a therapist to help her rediscover her identity and relocate her backbone, so to speak. It helped. As she changed, he adapted. Things are better, if not ideal. I wonder what would have happened if her husband hadn't responded positively to her transformation and if she had continued to languish in a marriage bereft of mutuality.

In all my reading, research, and reflection about marriage, one quality has stood out, head and shoulders above all others, as the hallmark of a healthy relationship. It's so obvious that it's easy to overlook, tempting to undervalue. It's kindness. (I am beginning to worry that I will sound like a broken record.) I can't help but wonder if, in the context of marriages between Christians, kindness might flow into the holy risk of mutual submission.

It's tempting to roll our eyes at this. If it were that easy, we might say, then why aren't there more strong, stable, loving relationships? Why do so many marriages limp along unhappily or end in painful divorce? But here's the thing: practicing kindness and mutuality isn't easy at all. It's work. It's *hard* work. It's listening when you don't feel like listening. It's compromising when you'd really rather have your way. It's relentlessly considering the well-being and desires of someone other than yourself and resisting the inherent impulse we human beings have toward selfishness.

Just for the sake of discussion, let's set aside the question of gender for a moment. I do not mean to say there aren't differences between men and women, whether instilled by nature or nurture. I simply believe that this passage has a good word about marriage regardless of whether any given wife subscribes to traditional ideas about femininity or any given husband is the family breadwinner. I believe this passage has a good word for marriage, period, regardless of gender. Which is to say that I think the depth and flexibility of this biblical wisdom applies to marriages of two men or two women just as readily as it applies to marriages made of a wife and a husband.

I am not going to pretend that marriage is not a complicated thing. There are countless ways for marriages to thrive, and there are countless ways for marriages to fail. But I suspect that the presence or absence of mutuality and kindness is, at the very least, a very prominent part of the pattern. It takes a willingness to risk, to be vulnerable, to be subject to the other.

I also think of my new friend Felicity. She's about half a generation younger than I am, and is newly engaged to Joshua. Despite her brevity of years, and although she has not yet actually experienced marriage, her grasp of mutuality in marriage is astounding. She teaches me. Refined in the fires of a fundamentalist college that preached strict complementarianism, Felicity has come to understand this about marriage:

> It comes down to this for me: God is telling the story of redemption. He is calling the world back to himself, always has been. In all the unraveling, he is spinning up the spool again, putting chaos back in order, rebuilding the kingdom.

Part of the disorder—a huge part—is inequality. God has given us equal access to himself, he has chosen all of us to be heirs, all of us to be priests and priestesses in his kingdom. Complementarianism, to me, only prolongs the disorder that God is redeeming. It qualifies inequality—puts us into boxes to which God never relegated us.

Jesus, then, is how the disorder is being righted. And Jesus told us to drop everything and follow him. I don't follow my husband to him; I follow him. I sit at his feet, I learn, I lead, I teach, I preach. All of us do.

To be mutually submissive is to honor the person I marry as the person who sits beside me at the feet of Jesus. I recognize that Jesus has called us both. I want to love Joshua like Jesus loves, I want to serve him and carry him and push him and pull him and challenge him and apologize to him and cheer for him—and I know he wants to do the same for me.

Earlier in his letter to the Christians in Ephesus, before he begins handing out advice, Paul offers this prayer for his readers: "I pray that, according to the riches of his glory, he may grant that you may be strengthened in your inner being with power through his Spirit, and that Christ may dwell in your hearts through faith, as you are being rooted and grounded in love" (Ephesians 3:16-17).

This is my prayer for husbands and wives, complementarian or egalitarian. This is also my prayer for parents and children, for friends and neighbors—for all who seek to live and love faithfully.

20
VERY MARRIED

A friend's husband claims that infidelity is contagious—
and that if anyone in our social circle breaks their marriage vows, he's ousting them from the annual Thanksgiving
potluck. I suspect he's right, to a point; maybe it becomes
easier to justify an inappropriate relationship to yourself if
you know a good friend has engaged in similar extramarital
forays. But I also imagine that the reverse of his theory might
also be true. Fidelity can be catching too, if we have the courage to hold one another accountable to our promises.

Years ago, a friend—let's call her Kelly—dropped a rather
odd comment about a coworker while we were walking with
friends on the beach. Her comment led me to believe that
their relationship might be more than just innocuous chats in
between sales calls. I would tell you that I'm not one to pry,
but I would be lying through my teeth. I am *totally* one to
pry, and pry I did.

It turns out Kelly and Scott had begun hitting a nearby happy hour after work. It had started as a monthly outing with other colleagues, but one Tuesday afternoon Scott broadcast the "Who's up for Applebee's?" call and Kelly was the only one in the office who accepted the invitation. On her way to the bar, tailing Scott's sedan, Kelly felt a flicker of hesitation. Was it okay for a relatively newly married woman to get a beer with a bachelor? She pushed aside her concern. After all, they were just friends. They drank their drinks, they traded snarky comments about their officemates, they parted ways—Kelly to have dinner with her husband, Scott to his CrossFit class. (Reader, this is called characterization. You may accurately deduce that Scott was ripped.) Kelly didn't happen to mention to her husband that she'd had a drink alone with Scott, letting him presume that they had been in the company of other sales reps.

The following Tuesday, Scott sidled up to Kelly's cubicle and asked if she wanted to grab another drink. She did. Nothing happened. The following Tuesday, Scott issued an invitation that felt unnecessary; they had developed a standing date.

So when we met at the beach the next morning for walk with a group of girlfriends, Kelly mentioned Scott in a tone that set off my warning bells. The other women didn't seem ruffled as Kelly pondered aloud if she should be worried about her drinks with Scott. Hanging out with a colleague was no big deal, the group quickly reassured her. They did it all the time. So did their husbands. I wanted to join in the consensus. But I couldn't shake my suspicion that something was off. "Kelly," I said, glad we were walking so I didn't have to look her in the eye as I asked the question, "do you feel uncomfortable because you think you might have feelings for him?"

All chatter ceased. During the tense pause that followed I mentally kicked myself for having asked the question in front of our other friends. It's bad enough to pry, but to pry in public? Too rude.

I glanced at Kelly out of the corner of my eye; her eyes were fixed on the Palos Verdes Peninsula, an inscrutable expression on her face. "Yes," she said quietly.

Another pause followed, this one less tense than confused. I'm convinced that people are not well equipped to hold one another accountable. This might be especially true of women. One of the best pieces I've ever read from the satirical masters at the *Onion* was a feature about women spending a "raucous" night validating one another: "As the women moved from one bar to the next, the evening reportedly only grew more and more wild, with the friends telling one another whatever they needed to hear regarding callous comments made by boyfriends, deteriorating relationships with family members, pet deaths, or frustrating new haircuts."[1] It's cringeworthy because it's true. The social pressure to offer unwavering and unquestioning support to our female friends—even if we think they are actually in the wrong—is intense. When Kelly divulged that she had spent the last three Tuesdays evenings with a cute guy from work, the impulse to affirm that the dates were innocuous was fierce. When Kelly admitted her romantic feelings, her girlfriends were suddenly unable to simply tell her what she wanted to hear.

A remarkable conversation followed. Kelly's initial confession led to secondary admissions: Yes, they had definitely
been flirting. Yes, he had asked if she wanted to go home
with him. No, they hadn't kissed. No, she hadn't said a word
to her husband. By the time we finished our walk, Kelly's
girlfriends had helped her come up with a fairly comprehen-
sive plan to retreat from the dangerous territory in which she
found herself. She wasn't in a position to quit her job, so she
had to find a way to work with Scott without continuing the
flirtation. No more happy hours, obviously. And she would
ask a friend to swap clients with her to avoid going on a
business trip with Scott; people swapped for calendar reasons
all the time, so we helpfully invented an extremely important social engagement that meant she couldn't possibly go to
Orlando the week after Easter. She wasn't ready to broach
the subject with her husband, but agreed to the suggestion
one of our friends lifted up: sit on it for a week, create some
distance between herself and Scott, and then decide if it was
time to tell her husband.

As far as I know, Kelly never did cheat on her husband,
nor tell him that she considered doing so. The matter continued to come up for the next few weeks as we checked in
with Kelly to see how her plan was proceeding. Not long
after their third and final happy hour, Scott left their company for another job. Kelly was relieved beyond measure. His
departure meant it was truly over. It's been years since I've
seen Kelly, but she's still married; her last Christmas letter
announced the birth of their fifth child.

I have carried that story with me for years. It struck me
as a powerful testimony to the influence of healthy, honest,

open friendships. During weddings, the gathered community promises to support the couple in their marriage, but I reckon we don't always know what this looks like in practice. Sometimes it looks like this: a small band of exercise walkers being a little bit rude and a little bit wise as they guide one of their number away from temptation.

I may not have noticed the warning signs of my own near miss if I didn't have Kelly's story tucked in my memory, and I would have had a considerably harder time staying on the narrow path if not for the friends who walked with me when it was my turn to flirt with flirtation.

I first encountered Jen when she was a panelist at a conference several years ago. I was taken by her affable demeanor and wisdom. When she mentioned, almost as an aside, that she wanted to be "a person who is excellent to the people in my life," I thought to myself, *Gee, I'd like to be a person in her life.* Somehow I managed, without being too obviously stalkerish, to do just that. A couple of years later, at the same conference, we found ourselves camped out by the food table at an otherwise merry reception for writers, clutching our wine glasses and discussing the joys and challenges of marriage.

I was in a state, still working out my angst at having recently encountered temptation. I sorely needed the perspective of a friend who had remained happily married, through seasons both fair and stormy, for a quarter of a century. I spilled my guts (and my wine, but that's immaterial). Jen received my emotional unloading with grace and empathy. It wasn't exactly the small talk and networking in which I had expected to be engaged—and thank God for that. It was one of a handful of conversations that saved my marriage and therefore, as far as I am concerned, my life.

Marriage was once again on the table some time later as Jen and I chatted over cappuccinos and sandwiches at a café kitty-corner from a towering Gothic Revival church. It was a bright but frigid midwinter afternoon, and the sun shone in my eyes as we talked about the ways evolving theologies of sexuality and marriage had wracked her beloved church—the big one across the street. Like many Episcopal congregations, hers had been deeply divided by the 2003 election of the Right Reverend Gene Robinson, an openly gay priest, to the role of bishop of New Hampshire. The church was eviscerated—spiritually, emotionally, and financially—when conservative parishioners left en masse. Jen lost beloved friends. While she still loves and serves the church, more than a decade later she still aches when she remembers all the ugliness.

We also talked about the article on temptation, covenant, and fidelity I had just published in the *Christian Century*. I could hardly believe that I'd really done it. My first draft of the piece was cast as Christian fiction. I rechristened myself as a curly-haired youth minister named Martha, invented entirely divergent identities for the principal characters, and exaggerated the plot to approximate an actual affair. The copy on the book flap when my debut novel hit the stores would be titillating but circumspect for its intended Christian readers: *Martha's happy marriage to a boorish bank teller is jeopardized when she realizes she has fallen for a megachurch pastor she met at a worship conference! Will she honor her vows to Michael, or will she throw it all away for an adulterous affair with Joel? Only God knows . . .*

The amateur-hour fiction I wrote felt far safer than actually claiming the story as my own. Though I'd written about fairly personal matters in the past, surely I could never actually publicly admit to having dallied near the precipice of adultery. Telling a friend? Yes, of course. Telling anyone who happened to click through or pick up a copy of the magazine? The stuff of my worst nightmares. Yet I ultimately couldn't resist the temptation to tell the story of temptation resisted. In a culture saturated with stories of infidelity, my story of fidelity wanted to be told.

I felt sick the day the essay went live online; I sat in my study physically shaking, panicked. What had I done? I wanted to burn every last print copy and hack the server to destroy the digital evidence. I had received Benjamin's blessing, of course. I wouldn't have published it otherwise. But would his feelings change once it was out there for all the world to see? What would my church think? Even in congregations that don't put clergy on pedestals, people don't necessarily want to know their married preacher had the hots for a dude she met at [redacted for the privacy of all relevant parties]. And then there was the unsettling reality that despite my best attempts to veil the identity of my friend, writing about the matter publicly meant that at some point I would likely be faced with the profoundly awkward question of whether I would come clean to him—and his wife. My friend did eventually read and recognize himself in the essay. He contacted me to cautiously inquire if he had figured right—not for motives of prurience or vanity, but for a noble reason: in my abundance of caution, I'd kept him at enough of a distance that he had sadly concluded he must have done something to offend me. My revelation was his absolution. Before I responded, I conferred with Benjamin. "I love you and I trust you," he replied. With my husband's love as my anchor and his trust as my shield, I responded; I could not in good conscience lie. I suspect that ninety-nine times out of a hundred it's best not to divulge having had feelings for someone for whom one has no business having feelings, but in this case it was the right thing to do.

Further complicating matters: as if to rub my misgivings in my face, the universe thoughtfully arranged to make my essay go viral. Not "fly me out to the *Today* show" viral, but viral nonetheless. In addition to the mind-boggling traffic the essay generated, conversations about fidelity, temptation, and covenant cropped up in pockets throughout social media and, I've been told, across kitchen tables. As it turned out, readers were eager for a story that was not about infidelity, but about fidelity in the face of temptation. Just days after I fought my irrational impulse to bury the essay, I received an invitation to consider writing the very volume you hold in your hands.

I discussed my fears and my timid excitement with Jen. Could I really consider the possibility of taking on such an ambitious, intimidating project? She hesitated for a moment before responding. "Be careful," she warned. "Be very careful." Apparently Jen did not get the memo that girlfriends are supposed to tell you what you want to hear.

My brilliant and theologically liberal friend sheepishly started talking about spiritual warfare—you know, the idea that supernatural powers of good and evil are constantly duking it out. To cover my surprise, I kept eating the

double-fudge brownie I'd ordered, polishing off the whole
thing even though it was roughly the size of my head.

Jen was dead serious. She had noticed a pattern in her
own work. When she wrote about something in her life, she
felt as though it was getting, for lack of a better explanation, "attacked." When she was composing an article about
parenting tips, for instance, her kids would act out in ways
that made her question if she had any right to claim any wisdom about childrearing. Similarly, her spiritual life stalled
out while she worked on a book of devotional essays. She'd
developed resistance to this over the years; otherwise, she'd
never have the courage to continue writing such honest and
lovely pieces about parenting and faith. But she was worried about me, and about my marriage—the marriage that
she had been so instrumental in redeeming not long before.
Could Benjamin and I weather whatever tribulations a project like this might dredge up, supernatural or otherwise?

Jen's words were sobering. I trust her, and look up to her,
and have the utmost respect for her opinion. For this and
a whole host of reasons, practical and cowardly, I nearly
said no.

But here we are. And it wasn't the gentle persistence of the
acquisitions editor that won me over. Not really. Marriage
is, for better or for worse (for richer and for poorer?), one of
the things I feel called to write about, no matter how reluctantly I may do so. I've long been drawn to the notion that
marriage can be a sort of home base for ministry in the world
beyond your doorstep. This takes different forms, of course.
A fraction of married couples are literally missionaries, living
and working overseas or in decaying urban neighborhoods.

But there are far less obvious yet far more common ways that healthy marriages can be a blessing beyond the nuclear family. Most couples are engaged in vocations that don't have an overt connection to the life of faith, yet their marriages grant them a foundation from which to practice hospitality, nurture community, and be good neighbors.

One reason I keep writing about our marriage is because Benjamin keeps encouraging me to do so. Indeed, my husband is the one who first proposed that I write about our relationship. He sensed before I did that sharing a portion of our journey might be a worthwhile endeavor, even though an honest account of our life together requires us both to face brokenness we might rather sweep out of sight. He helps me trust that this is all worth it, that using the broken pieces to create something beautiful is redemptive for us and potentially a source of wisdom and encouragement for others. My husband's willingness to let me tell our story is one of the things that truly flabbergasts me about him. I have struggled mightily with the vulnerability of personal writing, but I'd choose narrating my own story over being a character in somebody else's version of the truth any day. But my husband wants to be of service even when it costs him a portion of his pride. He has helped me see that what I do on the page is a form of testimony. In bearing witness to our flawed but faithful marriage, I—we—hope to point to the love of God, the work of the Holy Spirit, and the Christ whose grace is sufficient and whose power is made perfect in weakness. What is testimony but a glad boasting of weakness so that the power of Christ the Word may dwell among us anew?

One certainly needn't be a writer to bear testimony to the blessings and burdens of marriage. With all due respect to the marriage counselors and family therapists who offer professional support to couples in crisis, I suspect as many or more marriages are salvaged by ordinary people who are willing to share their wisdom and stories with their friends.

Weeks after our lunch date, knowing I was leaning toward signing the contract that would legally bind me to tell our story, Jen sent me a long email, reiterating how protective she felt toward me, and toward my marriage. She encouraged us to consider how writing the book might affect our marriage, and to be prepared for whatever "negative whatnots" that might come our way. We should have more date nights; we should have more sex. "Don't let it negatively affect the beautiful, resilient marriage you are making," the note concluded. I forwarded it to Benjamin. Even if he hadn't already been on board, the promise of extra romps in the hay with his wife might have been enough to elicit his enthusiastic endorsement.

We are indeed making a beautiful and resilient marriage together, and writing this book has seemed to help, not hurt, our relationship. Fixing my attention on our ever-lengthening love story has been a gift to me and to my marriage. The honesty, integrity, and accountability it has taken to commit our relationship to the page has felt very much like a public renewal of covenant. It's made me more keenly aware that our love story—like every good love story—has eternal significance. We love because God first loved us. We will continue to fall short of our intentions to be paragons of patience and kindness and mutuality. But we will also continue to do whatever it takes to remain joyfully, faithfully, and *very* married.

We have come so far. We have so far to go. Thank God we are not alone.

EPILOGUE

We slip into Last Exit Books just as Benjamin's old friend Steve starts reading a poem. We're late for the Jawbone Poetry Open; miles of construction along the route from Illinois to Ohio delayed our arrival. We stopped at my parents' house just long enough to drop off the girls and then took the back roads to Kent. Our college town has changed dramatically, but the rural landscape that surrounds it hasn't. The same horse stable, the same railroad tracks, the same ramshackle white farmhouse on the corner of Johnson Road. And, as we enter the circle of folding chairs, the same poets. Some I know only by face and voice. Others, by name: Maj, Alice, David.

Steve. It's been fifteen years since he announced, on a boulevard in Chicago, that it would take a special woman to marry Benjamin. When he finishes reading his poem, he looks up and lights up, happy to see us.

I am listening to the voices of the readers but I am also writing a poem in my head. It opens with this scene: Benjamin and I lowering ourselves into a two-person kayak and launching into the brilliant blue waters of the Pacific Ocean. We are young. My hair is still bleached an impossible shade of blonde. I am not yet a mother. We tool around the harbor, paddling as close to the seals as we dare. I point the craft toward the open ocean, past the safety of the harbor wall. When we cross over, Benjamin panics. The enormity of the ocean's depth, even this close to shore, undoes him. He wants to return to the harbor.

I resist. I am loving every moment. When Benjamin turns around to implore me to help steer the kayak back to safety, he sees that I am grinning. The smile infuriates my husband. I cannot convince him of the truth. I am insensitive, yes, enjoying the thrill of the waves while my beloved sinks into dread. But I insist that I am not laughing at him.

We bicker viciously. The day is ruined. We return the kayak to the rental shop early.

The second scene unfolds years later. We are kayaking again, this time on the relative safety of a Wisconsin lake. We could drown just as easily in these depths, but the calm green freshwaters aren't fearsome. We are each in our own kayaks this time. After the fiasco in and just beyond the Redondo Beach harbor, I spitefully declared that we were constitutionally unfit to share a kayak.

We glide along the surface of the lake, hewing close to the wooded banks, stopping every so often to squint at a bald eagle. By the time we turn around to head back to camp, I'm starting to tire. We immediately discover we've made a classic mistake: not realizing that the wind had been at our backs. The return trip is arduous. My arms tire, my shoulders ache, and my lower back, susceptible as it is to pain and spasms, protests.

I wish, more than anything, that I were in the same kayak as my husband.

My reverie is interrupted when I realize, with a start, that I recognize the words being spoken by one of the old-timers. She's quoting from "A Wedding Story for Ben and Katherine." A phrase here, an image there. I press my elbow into Benjamin's rib. Christ Episcopal Church, where we first heard Maj read these words, is just down the way, on the other side of the Cuyahoga River.

When she folds her papers and falls silent, Steve leans toward us. "That was half your wedding poem, right?" he says.

The poet, meanwhile, adds a footnote giving credit to her sources. "Rumi and Ragain," she says, with a laugh. Maj chuckles too, teasing her for stealing his poem. Our poem.

Benjamin clears his throat and reads the devotional he wrote for our church's last Lenten series. In it, he tells the story of how he used to climb through Steve's window at night and crash on his couch. Steve never got angry or locked him out. He would bake corn bread to give to Benjamin for breakfast. "I needed that open window. I needed a place to crash where a friend was in the other room. I don't think that I understood at the time how desperate I was to not be alone."

"Life is better now," he reads.

My friend John Blase says that to be married is to be "unusually dependent." I like this. It reminds me of people who scoff at religion as a crutch. There's no shame in needing crutches to walk.

There's no shame in needing covenant to live.

ACKNOWLEDGMENTS

Valerie Weaver-Zercher, Amy Gingerich, and all the people at Herald Press and MennoMedia: thank you. *(Without you, there would have been no book.)*

Eugene H. Peterson: thank you. *(I still can't believe you said yes.)*

Maj Ragain: thank you. *(Let's swap some poems on that new back porch.)*

Lara Bolger: thank you. *(What would I do without you?)*

My dear Reverent Writers: Bromleigh McCleneghan, Lee Hull Moses, Heidi Haverkamp, Jenn Moland-Kovash, and Erica Schemper: thank you. *(The longer the email chain, the better.)*

Amy Julia Becker and Alan Van Wyk: thank you.
(You went above and beyond.)

Rachel Marie Stone, Jennifer Grant,
and Caryn Rivadeneira: thank you.
(Wise women.)

Tracey Bianchi, Dale Hanson Bourke, Micha Boyett,
Gina Dalfonzo, Andrea Dilley, Ellen Painter Dollar,
Lesa Engelthaler, Susy Flory, Marlena Graves,
Alison Hodgson, Keri Wyatt Kent, Helen Lee, Anita Lustrea,
Gillian Marchenko, Jessica Mesman, Jen Pollock Michel,
Sharon Hodde Miller, Karen Swallow Prior,
Melinda Correa Schmidt, Laura Turner, Halee Gray Scott,
and Michelle Van Loon: thank you.
(Y'all are proof that virtual space can be sacred space.)

Don Ottenhoff, Michael McGregor,
Lauren F. Winner, and all the people I've met
through the Collegeville Institute: thank you.
(Meet me at Stumpf Lake?)

All the staff and members of First Congregational
Church of Western Springs: thank you.
(I'm so lucky to be one of your pastors.)

Moms in Faith: thank you.
*(When the prospect of writing for an unknown readership
is too daunting, you're the ones I imagine reading my
words. In a very literal way, I wrote this book for you.)*

Rich Kirchherr and Clare Kralovec-Kirchherr: thank you.
(Beloved mentors, dear friends.)

Bridget Sperduto: thank you.
*("Happy is the woman who meditates on wisdom
and thinks intelligently, who ponders in her heart on
wisdom's ways and secrets" [Sirach 14:20-21, adapted].)*

Anna and Ben Roberts: thank you.
(It doesn't seem possible that we aren't actually family.)

Lisa Hofmann: thank you.
(Always.)

Morgan Meis and Stefany Anne Golberg: thank you.
*(You are still, in my mind,
the pink Himalayan salt of the earth.)*

My United Church of Christ clergy cohort, especially
Elizabeth Dilley and Jeanne Murawski: thank you.
*(Grateful to belong in your midst,
even as I cling to my Disciple roots.)*

Steve Thorngate, Richard Kauffman, and all the
fine people at the *Christian Century*: thank you.
(Writing for the Christian Century
is an honor that never gets old.)

Tsh Oxenreider: thank you.
*(Writing for The Art of Simple is
also an honor that never gets old.)*

Glennon Doyle Melton: thank you.
(Love wins.)

Nish Weiseth, Megan Tietz, Sarah Bessey,
and all the people who taught me that being
brave means telling the Deeper Story: thank you.
(I still miss us.)

Ed Cyzewski: thank you.
(You are a pastor to writers.)

Kelly Flanagan: thank you.
(You help us tell a better story.)

Karin Bergquist and Linford Detweiler: thank you.
(For the music, et cetera.)

The Persheys: thank you.
(I'm glad to be one of you.)

My sisters: thank you.
(I'm sorry those bridesmaid dresses were so terrible.)

Richard and Beverly Willis: thank you.
(Married more than fifty years. Wow.)

Juliette and Genevieve: thank you.
(I promise I'll try to write a children's book, someday.)

Ben: thank you.
(Obviously.)

NOTES

FOREWORD

1. Jeanne Murray Walker, "Sacrifice," in *A Deed to the Light* (Champaign: University of Illinois Press, 2004), 17.

2. Emily Dickinson, "Renunciation—Is a Piercing Virtue," in *The Complete Poems of Emily Dickinson* (New York: Little, Brown, 1961), 745.

3. Eugene H. Peterson, *Where Your Treasure Is: Psalms That Summon You from Self to Community* (1993; repr., Grand Rapids: William B. Eerdmen's, 2001), 180.

1. WANDER AS I WONDER

1. Sandra Tsing Loh, "Let's Call the Whole Thing Off," *Atlantic*, July/August 2009, http://www.theatlantic.com/magazine/archive/2009/07/lets-call-the-whole-thing-off/307488/.

2. Elizabeth Gilbert, *Committed: A Skeptic Makes Peace with Marriage* (New York: Viking, 2010), 5.
3. Ibid., 264–65.
4. Pamela Haag, *Marriage Confidential* (New York: Harper Collins), 20.
5. Kate Braestrup, *Marriage and Other Acts of Charity: A Memoir* (New York: Little, Brown, 2010), 6.
6. "About the Sexperiment," The Sexperiment, accessed June 2, 2016, https://thesexperiment.com/about-sexperiment.
7. Sarah Zylstra, "Are Evangelicals Bad for Marriage?" *Christianity Today*, February 14, 2014, http://www.christianitytoday.com/ct/2014/february-web-only/are-evangelicals-bad-for-marriage.html.
8. Obergefell v. Hodges, 14–556 U.S., slip op. at 28 (2015), http://www.supremecourt.gov/opinions/14pdf/14-556_3204.pdf.

2. IN WANT OF A HUSBAND

1. Douglas Martin, "Mildred Loving, Who Battled Ban on Mixed-Race Marriage, Dies at 68," *New York Times*, May 6, 2008, http://www.nytimes.com/2008/05/06/us/06loving.html.
2. Stephanie Coontz, *Marriage, A History: How Love Conquered Marriage* (New York: Penguin Books, 2005), 95.

4. IF I KNEW THEN

1. Sarah Bessey, "Damaged Goods," *Sarah Bessey* (blog), February 2, 2015, http://sarahbessey.com/ damaged-goods/; originally published on A Deeper Story, January 29, 2013.

2. Ibid.

3. Timothy Keller with Kathy Keller, *The Meaning of Marriage: Facing the Complexities of Commitment with the Wisdom of God* (New York: Penguin, 2013), 82.

4. David Brooks, "The Power of Marriage," *New York Times*, November 22, 2003, http://www.nytimes.com /2003/11/22/opinion/the-power-of-marriage.html.

5. Keller, *Meaning of Marriage*, 83.

6. Gerald W. Schlabach, "What Is Marriage Now?" *Christian Century*, October 20, 2014, http:// www.christiancentury.org/article/2014-10/ what-marriage-now.

5. NEEDING THE VOWS

1. Dietrich Bonhoeffer, *Letters and Papers from Prison*, Dietrich Bonhoeffer Works 8 (Minneapolis: Fortress Press, 2010), 84.

2. Code of Canon Law, c. 1095, in *Code of Canon Law: Latin-English Edition* (Washington, DC: Canon Law Society of America, 1998), http://www. vatican.va/archive/ENG1104/_P3Z.HTM.

3. Stephen Macedo, *Just Married: Same Sex Couples, Monogamy, and the Future of Marriage* (Princeton, NJ: Princeton University Press, 2015), 112.

4. Andrew J. Cherlin, *The Marriage-Go-Round: The State of Marriage and the Family in America Today* (New York: Alfred A. Knopf, 2009), 9.

5. Ibid., 4.

6. HOMEWARD CRAWL

1. *"Welcome Home,"* Gurdon Brewster Sculptor, accessed June 2, 2016, http://www.gurdonbrewster.com/gbwelcomehomecrosslarg.html.

2. Beyoncé Knowles Carter, *Lemonade* (Parkwood Entertainment 2016), video, 65 min.

3. Tamara Hill Murphy, "Beyoncé's *Lemonade*: No Rush to Forgiveness," *Think Christian*, April 26, 2016, https://thinkchristian.reframemedia.com/beyonces-lemonade-no-rush-to-forgiveness.

4. Esther Perel, "After the Storm," *Psychotherapy Networker*, July/August 2010, https://www.psy-chotherapynetworker.org/magazine/article/430/after-the-storm.

5. William S. Burroughs, *The Letters of William S. Burroughs, vol. 1, 1945–1959* (New York: Penguin Books, 1994), 213.

7. BLESSING UPON BLESSING

1. Universal Life Church Online homepage, accessed June 2, 2016, http://www.ulc.net/.

2. 31. "Become Ordained," Universal Life Church Online, accessed June 2, 2016, http://www.ulc.net/index.php?page=ordain.

9. LONG OBEDIENCE

1. Robert Sheer, "Playboy Interview: Jimmy Carter," *Playboy*, March 7, 2006, https://www.playboy.com/articles/playboy-interview-jimmy-carter; originally published November 1976.

10. FOR THOSE WHO MEANT FOREVER

1. Ann Patchett, *This Is the Story of a Happy Marriage* (New York: Harper Perennial, 2013), 69.
2. "Order for the Recognition of the End of a Marriage," *Book of Worship* (Cleveland: United Church of Christ, 2006), 289.
3. Ibid., 293.

11. FLUNKING EPHESIANS 4:26

1. Eavan Boland, "Domestic Violence," in *Domestic Violence* (New York: W. W. Norton, 2007).
2. "25 Statistics on Domestic Violence," Ohio Domestic Violence Network, accessed February 13, 2016, http://www.odvn.org/Uploads/Documents/25%20STATS%20corrected%202%20final.pdf.
3. Joe Johnson, "Athens Prosecutor, Domestic Violence Advocates Seek to Make Strangulation a Felony," *Athens Banner Herald*, December 6, 2013, http://onlineathens.com/local-news/2013-11-24/athens-prosecutor-domestic-violence-advocates-seek-make-strangulation-felony.
4. Richard Paul Evans, "How I Saved My Marriage," *HuffPost Weddings*, May 30, 2015, http://www.huffingtonpost.com/richard-paul-evans/how-i-saved-my-marriage_b_6958222.html.

5. Emily Esfahani Smith, "Masters of Love," Atlantic. com, June 12, 2014, http://www.theatlantic.com/ health/archive/2014/06/happily-ever-after/372573/.

6. Diane Stark, "Tween Crushes," *Thriving Family*, February/March 2015, http://www.thrivingfamily. com/Family/Stages/Tween%20Ages/2015/tween-crushes.aspx.

13. THE SAME CHOICE

1. Wesley Hill, *Spiritual Friendship: Finding Love in the Church as a Celibate Gay Christian* (Grand Rapids: Brazos Press, 2015), 79.

2. Ibid., 82.

14. *MEMENTO MORI*

1. Mary Oliver, "The Summer Day," in *New and Selected Poems* (Boston: Beacon Press, 1992).

15. THERE IS MERCY

1. Sheldon Vanauken, *A Severe Mercy* (San Francisco: HarperSanFrancisco, 1977), 35.

2. Ibid., 39.

16. THE HEM OF JOY'S GARMENT

1. Louis C. K., "Countdown to Sorrow," YouTube video, 2:49, posted by James Cameron, January 1, 2014, https://www.youtube.com/watch?v=1sH-Qx-AJMnQ.

17. WHEN JUSTICE ROLLS DOWN

1. Stephen Macedo, *Just Married: Same-Sex Couples, Monogamy, and the Future of Marriage* (Princeton, NJ: Princeton University Press, 2015), 113.
2. Ibid., 114.
3. Robert Pear and David D. Kirkpatrick, "Bush Plans $1.5 Billion Drive for Promotion of Marriage," *New York Times*, January 14, 2004, http://www.nytimes.com/2004/01/14/us/bush-plans-1.5-billion-drive-for-promotion-of-marriage.html.
4. JoAnn Hsueh, Desiree Principe Alderson, Erika Lundquist, Charles Michalopoulos, Daniel Gubits, David Fein, and Virginia Knox, "Early Impacts from the Supporting Healthy Marriage Evaluation," MDRC, February 2012, http://www.mdrc.org/publication/early-impacts-supporting-healthy-marriage-evaluation.
5. Andrew J. Cherlin, *The Marriage-Go-Round: The State of Marriage and the Family in America Today* (New York: Alfred A. Knopf, 2009), 170.
6. Ralph Richard Banks, *Is Marriage for White People? How the African American Marriage Decline Affects Everyone* (New York: Dutton, 2011), 11.
7. Ibid., 12.
8. To learn more about Rev. Thames, find her on Twitter at @TsThames.

18. YOKED TO ANOTHER FAMILY

1. Mindy Kaling, *Is Everyone Hanging Out Without Me? (And Other Concerns)* (New York: Three Rivers Press, 2011), 165.

19. SUBJECT TO ONE ANOTHER

1. "New Study Finds That Egalitarian Marriage Doesn't Make Women Happier," *Wintery Knight* (blog), October 22, 2012, http://winteryknight.com/2012/10/22/study-finds-that-egalitarian-marriage-doesnt-make-women-happier/.
2. Sarah Bessey, *Jesus Feminist* (New York: Howard Books, 2013), 76.
3. Claire M. Powell, "[Ephesians] Commentary," in *The IVP Women's Bible Commentary*, ed. Catherine Clark Kroeger and Mary J. Evans, (Downers Grove, IL: InterVarsity Press, 2002), 703.
4. Ibid., 703–4.
5. Ibid, 704.

20. VERY MARRIED

1. "Female Friends Spend Raucous Night Validating the Living S--- Out of Each Other," *Onion*, February 23, 2012, http://www.theonion.com/article/female-friends-spend-raucous-night-validating-the--27446.

THE AUTHOR

Katherine Willis Pershey is author of *Any Day a Beautiful Change* and an associate minister of the First Congregational Church in Western Springs, Illinois. Her work has appeared in the *Christian Century* and the anthology *Disquiet Time* as well as on The Art of Simple. She and her husband, Benjamin, have two daughters.

Find discussion questions for this book at www.HeraldPress.com/StudyGuides, and connect with the author at www.katherinewillispershey.com.